John R. Parry

Nuts for Profit

A Treatise on the Propagation and Cultivation of Nut-bearing Trees adapted to successful Culture in the United States

John R. Parry

Nuts for Profit
A Treatise on the Propagation and Cultivation of Nut-bearing Trees adapted to successful Culture in the United States

ISBN/EAN: 9783337185756

Printed in Europe, USA, Canada, Australia, Japan

Cover: Foto ©Andreas Hilbeck / pixelio.de

More available books at **www.hansebooks.com**

NUTS FOR PROFIT

A TREATISE

ON THE

PROPAGATION AND CULTIVATION

OF

Nut-Bearing Trees

ADAPTED TO SUCCESSFUL CULTURE

IN THE

UNITED STATES

WITH EXTRACTS FROM LEADING AUTHORITIES

By JOHN R. PARRY,

PARRY, NEW JERSEY.

1897.

Copyrighted 1897, by
JOHN R. PARRY.

SINNICKSON CHEW,
PRINTER,
CAMDEN, NEW JERSEY.

PREFACE.

IN presenting this pamphlet, the object has been to, in a measure, gratify the cravings of the horticultural public on the subject of Nut Culture as the demand for this knowledge, through the great numbers of letters continually received, is evidence of the increasing interest manifested in this fascinating and profitable industry.

While I will not attempt to treat the entire list of Nuts that might be grown in the United States, I will confine myself to those most familiar in our markets and that can be produced at a profit.

As the cultivation of edible Nuts for commercial purposes in this country is yet in its infancy, and the literature on the subject very limited, and as Nuts, like pomaceous fruits, do not succeed equally well in all sections, I have drawn from the writings of the best authorities, as I have found them in the magazines and periodicals, which, together with my own observations, will give the experiences from various sections of the United States, and may be the better adapted to the localities and conditions of all.

Very Respectfully,

JOHN R. PARRY.

Parry, N. J., February, 1897.

...Nut Culture...

THE CULTURE OF NUT BEARING TREES FOR PROFIT IN the United States, except for timber, has until recently received but little attention. This is due largely to the abundance of wild nuts, which have partially supplied the market demand, but mainly from the fact that the trees have been but little grown in the nurseries, and those dug from the forests, or where they had come up naturally, having but little or no fibrous roots, their transplanting has been attended with much uncertainty, and the impression has been formed that the seed must be planted where the tree is intended to stand; while to the contrary, many of the nut bearing trees when grown in the nursery are well supplied with fibrous roots and can be transplanted as safely as an apple tree, and the planter has the benefit of three or four years' growth in the nursery over that of planting the seed, with the uncertainty of their coming up regularly, and the time, care and attention required to get them properly started.

For many years there has been some interest in planting nut bearing trees, both for shade and nuts. And we occasionally find on old farms, from which the original timber had been cut, the pioneers had spared the most valuable of the nut trees, consisting of Chestnut, Walnut, Shellbark and Pecan, which in succeeding years have yielded abundant crops of toothsome nuts that have not only gladdened the hearts of the younger generation in their annual gatherings and helped to while away the long winter evenings at the farmer's home, but have also proven a most valuable source of revenue during seasons of other crop failures. From these individual trees many have been stimulated to increase their planting and establish orchards of selected varieties.

As with fruit, great caution should be exercised in planting a nut orchard until a careful investigation has been made of the species best suited to soil and climate, and then select thrifty growing, productive varieties, the fruits of which are of large size, attractive appearance, good quality and ripening at the most desirable season to command ready sale at best prices. A safe plan in selecting the species for planting will generally be the productiveness, health and vigor of the trees and quality of nut of those planted or growing naturally in the neighborhood. And as nut trees cannot be depended on to reproduce themselves from seed, the only safe plan to establish an orchard of any desired variety is by perpetuation through the buds—by budding or grafting in their various forms by rooted layers or cuttings, or by suckers from roots of seedling trees.

HISTORY OF NUT CULTURE IN NORTH AMERICA.

As given by H. E. Van Deman, Ex-Pomologist, U. S. Department of Agriculture.

THE WILD NUTS of America were used as food by the aborigines long before the white man set foot on her shores. This is proven by specimens found buried in the graves of their dead. Captain John Smith mentions them in his history of the country as it was in his day, they being gathered by the Indians and eaten both raw and prepared in various ways. Acorn and Chestnut meal were common articles of use in the cookery of the ancient and modern squaws. To-day the western Indians use acorn meal made into cakes, and a sort of gruel.

After the occupation of the country by the present races, the principal use made of nuts by them was as a table luxury or delicacy eaten on festive occasions. Here and there a tree was left to stand in the fields when the forests were cut away, because of the choice nuts which it produced. Rarely were nut trees planted, and they more for ornament or shade than for their fruit.

The Persian Walnut, European Chestnut, and Hazel or Filbert, and the Almond were introduced in the early settlement of the country, but the culture of all these nuts was rarely and but feebly attempted. This was perhaps largely due to the fact that the wild, native trees of various kinds furnished an abundant supply for the limited demands for home and market use. But the increasing consumption of nuts in America, and the gradual destruction of the native trees for their timber, has induced a few persons to begin their culture in earnest. Not only is this true of the foreign species, but of the best of our native kinds. Although there are already many large orchards of nut trees of several kinds in America, the business may be said to be yet in its infancy.

At the present time there are large quantities of Chestnuts, Pecans, Hickorynuts, Walnuts, Chinquapins and Hazelnuts gathered and sold in the Eastern and Central States. In the mountains of the Southwest the Indians gather quantities of nuts from several species of the Pine. They are usually roasted about like Peanuts and are of very delicious flavor. They are on sale in many of the stores of those regions, and I have bought them of the Indians along the railroads in Arizona and New Mexico.

But a large portion of the nuts sold in our markets are imported from Europe, and this in the face of the fact that the most of them might be produced within our own borders. According to the reports of the United States government, for the fiscal year ending June 30, 1894, there were imported during that year nuts to the value of $1,463,899. Over half of this amount was paid for seven million four hundred and thirty-six thousand seven hundred and eighty-four pounds of Almonds. Of Cocoanuts there were $62,688 worth, and of all other nuts (which includes a few other tropical kinds, and the Chestnut, Persian Walnut and Filbert), there were $631,758 worth. The reports only mention the Cocoanut and Almond separately. There were exported nuts to the amount of $125,383; but as no further details of exported nuts are given, it is only possible to suppose that they were principally Pecans, Persian Walnuts, and probably a few Hickorynuts.

After a careful inspection of the warmest parts of Florida and California, I am convinced that the cocoanut will never be grown in the United States in any considerable quantities for market. Although I saw trees in Florida bearing very well, the area of their successful culture is small, and the transportation from the tropics is so cheap, that the price will probably be too low for successful competition on our part.

The Pecan

Of our wild nuts the Pecan is the best, and is gathered in larger quantities than any other. Its native habitat is the rich river and creek bottoms of the lower Mississippi valley. Texas produces the principal part of the crop sent to market. In the Fall of 1876 I saw many thousands of bushels brought to market there by the wagon load. In some of the cotton-growing sections of that State, as early as 1871, it is said that the Pecan crop was worth five times as much to the people as the cotton crop of that year. One authority states that in 1880, in the city of San Antonio alone, there were sold one million two hundred and fifty thousand bushels. Louisiana, Mississippi, Arkansas and Missouri also produce very good Pecans.

The selection of the choicest wild varieties for planting seedling orchards has been practiced to some extent for many years past. I saw standing near "the old Jackson battle-field," below New Orleans, two rows of majestic Pecan trees that were said to have some years borne over two barrels per tree. I judged them to have been planted over one hundred years ago. But it is not until within the last ten years that any considerable orchards have been set. These are principally in the Gulf States, where the Pecan succeeds much better than farther North.

The only sure way to propagate the varieties without degeneration is by budding or grafting, and this is being done by a very few advanced growers. Named varieties are being introduced, which have nuts twice as large as the common seedlings. Some of them have shells so thin as to be crushed in the bare hand, and with plump, sweet kernels.

The Chestnut The Chestnut is also highly esteemed at home and in the market. While the bulk of the quantity consumed by our people is supposed to be gathered from our forests, thousands of bushels are imported each year from France, Italy and Spain. There are four species of the Chestnut family growing within our borders. The one whose varieties are at present most largely used in orchard planting and in grafting into sprouts in old clearings is the European species. A few chance seedlings of this species in the Eastern States have for many years proven hardy in tree and abundant bearers of nuts of large size and good quality. Many seedlings from these trees have been grown and planted in orchards, but owing to their variability, grafting is resorted to by those who best understand the business. Some varieties of the Japanese species produce the largest of all Chestnuts, but they are usually of inferior flavor. I have within the past year seen some that were over six inches in circumference.

The wild native Chestnut is of sweeter and better flavor than all others, but the trees are not such early or abundant bearers, nor are the nuts as large. The most of those are of foreign parentage. However, the largest wild varieties are being sought out and grafted. Seedlings are also being grown, with the hope of getting kinds that will combine large size with other good qualities.

The Chinquapin, which is the smallest of the Chestnut family in all respects, is often found in the Eastern markets early in the Fall, as it is the first to ripen.

The Almond The Almond has been planted all over America for many years, and with high hopes of success; but it is now thoroughly proven that the edible varieties will not succeed east of the Continental divide, except near the Rio Grande. In the North they are tender, and in the South the bloom is killed by Spring frost, because it comes out too early. The hardy, hard-shelled varieties are worthless, because the kernels are not fit to eat.

In California there are many very large orchards of the Almond which produce large and profitable crops almost every year. Yet the statistics of that State show the product to be only about one-seventh of the amount consumed by our people. There is therefore abundant room for increased home production.

Better varieties have been grown from seed in California than the common kinds imported from Europe, and the nuts bring a high price in market. The outlook for the culture of the Almond is very encouraging in portions of California, Arizona, Utah and Idaho. It succeeds rarely in Nevada, New Mexico and Southwestern Texas.

The Persian Walnut Nuts of the Persian Walnut were brought at an early day from England and the Continent of Europe, where it had been introduced by the Greeks and Romans long before the Christian era. The Greeks first brought it from Persia, where it originally grew wild. Afterwards it escaped to the forests of Southern Europe. In America it is wrongly called "English" Walnut to distinguish it from our own species. The nuts planted by our forefathers grew and bore only fairly well in some cases because of lack of pollen, or the inopportune time of its production. This is now the chief cause of failure in many cases, and can be remedied by growing the right varieties contiguously.

The tree is not so hardy as those of our native Walnuts, but it is growing in the Atlantic States as far North as Massachusetts. In California large orchards are set. One is said to cover seven hundred acres. It is estimated that the annual crop of that State is now fully two million pounds. Successful culture demands a moderate climate, very rich, well drained land, and a steady supply of water, either naturally or artificially supplied. If the right varieties are judiciously planted, there is no reason to doubt the profitable culture of this nut in the Atlantic States from New Jersey southward.

The Hazel The Filbert, or European Hazel, has been grown only here and there in America, and in some cases with little success. The chief cause is the blooming of the staminate flowers, either too early or too late for the pistils. With some varieties there is no such trouble, and the bushes or small trees bear heavily. There is a bright future for the culture of the best varieties, especially in the Atlantic States and in Oregon and Washington.

Our wild Hazels furnish small nuts of good flavor, and the best varieties are now beginning to be propagated for experimental purposes.

The Hickory Nut The little Shellbark Hickory is a most valuable nut, and is gathered and sold wherever grown. The choicest varieties are being planted in a small way, and occasionally a few scions are grafted on stocks in the nursery or experimental grounds.

NUT CULTURE FOR NEW YORK.

By Prof. H. E. Van Deman, before the Western New York Horticultural Society.

OF THE many classes of fruits that may be successfully grown within the bounds of the Empire State, perhaps there is none that is more neglected by both market and amateur growers than nuts. For ages before the country was settled the natives have gathered wild nuts from the forests, and, since the white man has taken possession, he has done little so far to improve upon nature's methods of their culture. But there are good reasons for being encouraged to push the culture of some of the native wild species and also to plant some of the foreign kinds.

Chestnuts   Of the native species, the common Chestnut, *Castanea dentata*, is perhaps most promising of good results. There are thousands of trees bearing nuts of more than ordinary value, standing in open fields, that have been left because of this fact. Some of them bear nuts of large size, others are very productive, and all are of much better quality than nearly all of the foreign varieties, although smaller, and hence, less popular in market than the latter. Occasionally, trees are found which bloom abundantly but do not bear. Such cases occur nearly always where the trees stand alone and their barrenness is thought to be attributable to the staminate and pistillate flowers not coming to perfection at the same time, or to the impotency of their pollen; because, where two or more trees stand near each other, it rarely occurs.

Very little attention has so far been given to the production of choice seedlings or to the propagation by grafting of the best chance seedling varieties. Both of these methods could be practiced with decided advantage. There has been sufficient progress already made in the way of selecting and preserving from destruction by the ax, certain choice varieties, to furnish a fairly promising field of labor. A few of the best that have come under my personal notice and that have been deemed worthy of varietal names may be briefly mentioned:

Dulaney, Excelsior, Griffin, Hathaway, Murrell, Otto, and other choice varieties.

There are rocky hillsides and other waste patches already covered with young chestnut growth, that, by grafting, might be changed into groves of these and other choice varieties. Old timber slashings that have very young growth would be the best suited to such treatment.

European Chestnut For profitable planting at the present time, the European type, *Castanea sativa*, is the best species of Chestnut, all things considered. The trees of some of its varieties are somewhat tender in some sections of the United States, but numerous trials in New York have proven that there is little to be feared from this cause.

The nuts are large but of inferior flavor, compared with our wild Chestnuts, and some varieties have quite bitter skins covering the kernel, which must be removed before eating. Much less pubescence is found in the nuts than on those of our wild species. One objection that many practical men make to this species in nearly all its varieties, when worked on native American stocks, is that the union is not perfect and that winds are apt to break off the grafted top. There is considerable difference in this respect among the varieties; advantage can be taken of this, and only the most successful kinds worked upon the native stocks, either in the nursery or the wild sprouts in brush lands.

Mr. H. M. Engle, of Pennsylvania, told me very recently that he had more than forty acres of wild sprouts grafted principally to Paragon and the union seemed to be good in nearly all cases. He said that he had many grafted trees several inches in diameter, which were so perfectly healed at the graft that no evidence of the operation could be seen. I have seen such trees in several places.

If scions of varieties of the European type are set upon seedlings of the same species, there will be almost no uncongeniality of stock and scion. This can easily be done.

There are a goodly number of well tested varieties that have been so well thought of that they have long ago been named and are propagated in the nurseries by grafting and budding. Among them are the following: Paragon, Numbo, Ridgely, Hannum.

Japanese Chestnut The Japanese Chestnut, *Castanea Japonica*, has been thought by some to be only a variation of the European type, but there are sufficient points of difference to warrant botanists in giving it a separate specific name. The tree is smaller and so are the branches and leaves, but the nuts are generally large, and some of the varieties of this Asiatic species bear the largest of all Chestnuts, although some of them are quite small. Nearly all of them are of poor quality, and the skin is bitter, except in a few very rare cases. The nuts are, as a rule, almost devoid of pubescence. In point of bearing the trees are very precocious and productive. Unlike the European type the Japanese species of Chestnut usually succeed quite well worked upon our native American seedlings.

Mr. Luther Burbank, of California, has been for a long time growing seedlings of this species in the hope of securing choice varieties and has chosen two out of a lot of about ten thousand, that he considered good in all respects. These are now owned and being grafted extensively by two gentlemen in Connecticut.

A few chance seedlings, and some as the result of careful attempts to originate good varieties, have been thought to be worthy of varietal names and propagation by grafting. Some of these are mentioned below: Alpha, Early Reliance, Giant, Killen, Superb.

The Hickories Of the Hickory family there are only two species of special importance as nut trees anywhere in America, so far as we now know them. Of these, the Pecan, *Hicoria Pecan*, is out of climate in New York, being at home in the Gulf States and rarely doing well as a nut producing tree north of Delaware, Kentucky and Kansas. It will grow as far North as Southern Iowa and Massachusetts, but does not flourish in those States. It is by far the best of all native American nuts and already enters largely into commerce.

The Little Shellbark Next to the Pecan comes the Little Shellbark Hickory, *Hiciora ovata*, both in point of commercial importance and general goodness. It may seem strange to some, that there are firms in Pennsylvania that crate and ship kernels of this nut to the extent of twenty-three tons to a single season. Its range of natural territory is very large, extending from the New England States almost to the Gulf of Mexico. In most parts of New York it does well, as it is found wild in the forests and grown in many fields and pastures where the trees have been left because of the good qualities of their nuts. It might seem strange that the culture of this nut should be urged, but the steadily increasing destruction of the trees for their timber, and the increasing value of their nuts, would warn us to preserve all that may be practicable of the wild trees, and plant new Hickory groves. There are many waste places where little corners or rocky hillsides are already covered with Hickory growth that might be saved from the axe. Other places not easily cultivated might be planted with nuts of choice quality and thus made profitable. They should be planted about four feet apart each way and cultivated for a few years. As the trees grow they will need thinning to twenty-five or more feet apart, but the wood will abundantly pay for the labor and the young trees will keep down other growth. There is a great difference in the wild varieties of the Little Shellbark as regards size, thinness of shell, quality of the kernel and its readiness to part from the shell. There have been so few experiments with seedlings, that little is known as to the possibility of these good characteristics being generally transferred to them. Grafting is the only safe way according to present knowledge.

Within the past few years a number of choice varieties have come under my notice, and some of them have been named. No doubt there are many others equally good that should be brought to general knowledge. A few of the named kinds will be here mentioned: Hales, Leaming, Curtis, Eliot, Rice, Milford.

The Hazels

The nuts of the genus *Corylus* are called Hazelnuts, Filberts and Cobnuts rather indiscriminately in both Europe and America. All but one of these are of a rather shrubby nature, and propagate naturally by suckering.

American Hazels

Of this number, two are natives of a large part of Central North America, and are both found wild in some parts of New York. While their nuts are not so large as those of the European species, the flavor of their kernels is good, and the bushes are very hardy and productive. We mention the *Corylus Americana* and *Corylus Rostrata*.

European Hazels

There has long been considerable doubt and trouble about the proper classification of the three European species of the Hazel family, both to botanists and pomologists. They are a source of very considerable profit, chiefly in England, France, Italy and Spain. It is stated that many thousands of tons of Filberts and Cobnuts are annually exported from the county of Kent, England. Most varieties flourish best in a rather moist, cool and yet a mild climate.

In this country they have long been grown here and there over a wide area but in a very limited experimental way. One apparently serious obstacle to their successful cultivation here has been their liability to yield to the effects of fungous diseases. Experiments are now being made in New Jersey and elsewhere in the hope of finding remedies for this evil.

Another difficulty has been the inopportune time of the blooming of their staminate and pistillate flowers. This can be overcome by planting varieties near each other that will properly cross-fertilize. In Europe they sometimes cut branches from their wild hazel bushes that have pollen-bearing catkins, and hang them on the fruiting bushes for this purpose.

They are easily propagated by suckers, layers and cuttings, and also by grafting. Wet, heavy, rich soil will stimulate too strong a growth of wood and prevent fruitfulness. A poor sandy soil will make the nuts small and scarce. But a loose friable soil of moderate richness, and a well underdrained subsoil, seem to be well suited to Cobnut and Filbert culture. We believe that all the conditions suitable to their culture will yet be found in parts of New York.

Cobnut *Corylus Avellana*, is a species which is very common in Europe. In England its varieties are commonly called Cobnuts. Its habit is bushy, sometimes inclined to be tree-like and suckers freely at the base. The husk is two-parted, short and reflexed at maturity. The nuts are medium size, round or compressed and nearly always thin-shelled. There are several named varieties, of which the following are considered the best: Bond, Cosford, Downton Square and Pearson.

Filbert The nuts of the varieties of *C. Tubulosa* are commonly called Filberts. The habit of growth is stronger than that of the Cobnuts, being upright and with heavy branches, but suckers freely when not pruned into the shape of a small tree with a single stem. The husk is single-lobed, longer than the nut, and often contracted just above the nut. The nuts are elongated in shape, have thick shells, and the kernels are very richly flavored. There are a number of named varieties of excellent quality, from which the following are selected: Frizzled, Lambert, Purple, Red, White.

The Walnuts Of our native American Walnuts, there are none which at present seem to afford much opportunity for their profitable culture as nut bearing trees. Possibly the butternut, *Juglans Cinerea*, may yet develop varieties with shells thin enough, and meats large enough and of the right shape, to be easily extracted; but, as a rule, the shell holds the kernel too firmly in its crevices. The flavor is very rich and delicious. Crossing with other species may make new creations of peculiar value in all respects. That the tree is hardy in New York, we all know. It loves well drained upland slopes, and good deep soil.

Persian Walnut The species of the genus *Juglans*, which, up to this date, has been almost solely cultivated, is the Persian Walnut, *Juglans regia*, which in America has been improperly called English Walnut, because it was perhaps first brought to this country from England. It is a native of Asia, and was brought from Persia to Europe by the Greeks, who called it "Persian nut," and "Royal nut." The Romans having obtained it from the Greeks, called it "Juglans," which literally means "Jupiter's Acorn" or "nut of the gods." Wherever the Romans made conquests and established colonies they planted these nuts, and it was thus that the species was taken to England, where the Anglo-Saxons gave it the name "walnut," which means "foreign nut."

It is the best of all the family, but unfortunately in a large part of North America it is liable to injury by cold winters. In New York it is grown with difficulty and can scarcely be said to be successful. However, it may be wise to give it further trial in protected places.

As with other nut trees, there has been much trouble with the untimely blooming of the flowers of the two sexes, or a partial or entire lack of those producing pollen. Some varieties bloom so early as to be caught by frost. There are many named kinds of marked excellence, which have long been grown in France, and to some extent in other countries. If any attempt to cultivate this nut in New York the following varieties give promise of doing the best: Chaberts, Franquette, Mayette, Praeparturiens and Serotina.

Asiatic Walnuts

There are three species in this country, recently introduced direct from Asia, that are worthy of general trial in New York. They all seem to be hardy, thrifty and productive. Juglans Seiboldiana, J. Cordiformis, J. Mandchurica.

Hints on Grafting and Budding Nut Trees

There is no doubt that nut trees are hard to graft and bud, or, at least, that the proper methods are not well understood. Few persons have succeeded quite well, and so far as is known, this success is attributable to having practiced upon the following principles.

Evaporation of the sap or scion or bud should be prevented until the union has taken place with the stock. To accomplish this, it is best to hold back the scions by securely wrapping them in moss or other soft material and placing the package in a damp refrigerator or in the sawdust of an ice-house until the circulation of the sap in the stock has become active. Then, graft just under the ground and bank up with moist earth nearly to the top of the scion. All the work should be most carefully done. Waxing is not necessary in underground grafting, but in top grafting special care should be given to covering the wound thoroughly.

A very important point in preparing the scion for cleft grafting is, that the wedge should be so made that the pith is all on one side and not in the center of the wedge, as it usually is, for the large pith of nut trees will otherwise cause the scion to be fragile.

Ring-budding is much better than shield-budding for nut trees. In any style of budding the wrapping should be thoroughly done.

The Pecan and other Hickories will grow when grafted on each other. The European Chestnuts do best when grafted on seedlings of their own type. The same is true of the American species; but the Japanese kinds seem to do very well worked on our native stocks.

A PLEA FOR NUT TREES.

By A. S. Fuller, in American Agriculturist.

IT SEEMS to be one of the weaknesses of mankind to cling to old ideas, and even venerate the acts of ancestors, whether they were wise or otherwise. Because the first white men who settled in the New England States made much of the American elm, planting it almost everywhere to the exclusion of better and more valuable trees, or because the Holland Dutch, in the settlement of Manhattan and Long Island, saw fit to import Dutch cork-bark elm and European lindens, planting these about their grounds and along the roadsides, it does not follow that we should perpetuate their practices centuries later, as is now being done in many localities. In Europe this clinging to ancestral ideas and practices is just as much a trait of the people as it is in this country, but fortunately, some wise man of ancient times discovered that a tree might be both useful and ornamental, and, with the two combined, the planter would be doubly blessed.

When or by whom the Chestnut and Walnut were first introduced into Southern and Central Europe is now unknown, but it was very early discovered that they were beautiful and easily grown trees, yielding an immense amount of excellent and nutritious food for both man and beast. The fashion or custom once established among the people, the propagation and planting of these trees became general, and has continued uninterruptedly in several European countries for more than two thousand years. They are planted along the highways, in parks and forests, and for memorial trees for births and marriages—in fact, to set out a nut tree is considered an act commendable alike in prince and peasant. The result of this custom is to be seen in the annual crop of over thirty millions of bushels of Chestnuts alone, gathered in

France and Italy, and probably nearly or quite as many Walnuts. Hundreds of thousands of bushels of these nuts are exported, and we are pleased to obtain a share and pay a high price for them, although these nut trees will grow here as freely, and bear as abundantly, as in any country of Europe. They may not thrive in our extreme Northern border States, but they certainly do in many of the Northern, and all through the Middle or Southern States.

But it is not necessary to go to Europe or Asia for valuable nut-bearing trees, for our forests are full of them, and we have several native species worthy of extended cultivation. Our native Chestnut is superior to the foreign in flavor, although not as large, consequently does not command as high a price in the market, but it is becoming more and more valuable as the demand increases, and the supply decreases with the destruction of our original forests. The same is true of the Shellbark, Hickory and the Pecan nut, and all three should have long since been extensively planted as roadside trees in place of the hundreds of worthless varieties and species to be seen in such positions in all the thickly settled parts of our country. Of course where the European or Asiatic Walnut will thrive, and the larger varieties of the foreign Chestnut, we would give them a prominent position—not because they are more ornamental than the native kinds, but their nuts command a better price, and this is an incentive for planting and future care not to be ignored in any community nor under any circumstances.

It may take a little more time to secure a crop of nuts than of the ordinary kind of farm crops, but a nut tree, when large enough to yield from five to ten dollars' worth of nuts annually, will not occupy any more land than is required to produce a dollar's worth of wheat, or other kind of grain. In addition to this there is no annual plowing and seeding to be done for each ensuing crop, for when a nut tree is once established it is good for a hundred years or more, increasing in value and productiveness with age, and when, finally, its usefulness ends as a producer of food, its wood is worth as much as that of any of our purely ornamental trees. If our farmers and others, who were planting shade trees twenty-five and fifty years ago, had thought of this and put the idea to a practical test, the roadside trees alone would, to-day, yield many millions of dollars' worth of nuts, which we are compelled to obtain elsewhere.

Taking this view of the subject, I ask, in all sincerity, if it is not about time that a change was made in the kind of trees generally planted along our highways? Our ancestors in this country may have been very careless and unwise in the selection of the kinds of trees planted for such purposes, and, however much we may regret it, we should strive to remedy defects, keeping in mind that posterity will also have something to say about our plantings.

Mr. A. S. Fuller also says:

And further to show the extent to which they are imported to this country. Of Almonds, not shelled, and on which there is a protective duty of three cents per pound, we imported from 1890 to the close of 1893, twelve million four hundred and forty-three thousand eight hundred and ninety-five pounds, valued at $1,100,477.65; of Almonds, shelled, on which there is now a duty of five cents, we imported one million three hundred and twenty-six thousand six hundred and thirty-three pounds. The total value of both kinds for the four years amounted to $1,716,277.32.

Of Filberts and Walnuts, not shelled, and with a duty of two cents per pound, we imported during the same years from eleven to fifteen million pounds annually, or a total for the four years of fifty-four millions five hundred and twenty-six thousand one hundred and eighty-one pounds, and in addition about two million pounds of the shelled kernels, on which the duty was six cents (now four) per pound. The total value of these importations amounted to $3,176,085.34. Under the head of "miscellaneous nuts," or all other shelled and unshelled, "not specially provided for," which probably includes Chestnuts, there were imported during the period named, six million four hundred and forty-two thousand nine hundred and eight pounds, valued at $235,976.05. The total for all kinds of edible nuts imported was $7,124,575.82. These figures are sufficient to prove that we are neglecting an opportunity to largely engage in and extend a most important and profitable industry.

WILD & CULTIVATED NUTS.

From Southern Cultivator and Dixie Farmer.

THE DIVISION OF POMOLOGY, Department of Agriculture, will soon issue a bulletin upon the Wild and Cultivated Nuts of the United States.

In Central California, on well drained level lands, orchardists report cheering results with the hard and soft shell Almond. It is not an unusual thing to nd in that section plantations of from two thousand to five thousand of these trees. The culture is much the same as for the peach.

The Madeira nut is cultivated in orchards of from one hundred to fifteen hundred trees throughout the southern portion of California in proximity to the coast. By careful selection of seed and improved culture, seconded by a happy " sport " in nature, the growers of California have secured a very reliable " paper shell " variety of this nut. Reports of this " Improved " Madeira concur that it will bear in that locality at from five to seven years of age, that it has a very thin shell, and in kernel it surpasses the mother nut.

The Madeira is also reported from most of the States as among the collection of nut-trees grown by planting; its territory extends not quite so far south as the Pecan, nor so far north as the Shag-bark Hickory. On Staten Island, New York, the Madeira nut is marketed green for pickling and for catsup.

The Pecan is grown in orchards and in groves in the South Central and South Western States. By selection and culture there are now produced some very large soft-shell, superior nuts of this kind. While there are more Pecans grown in the native forests of the territory mentioned than in orchards, yet grove culture of this nut is profitable there, and promises an increased yield of larger and better nuts. The Pecan is very generally reported as far north as New York and west to the Missouri river.

As thorough and careful culture of this nut has not been reported by its propagators as is reported for the Almond and Madeira by their propagators, yet the nut shows decided improvement under the care and the attention given it.

The Shag-bark Hickory is not receiving any orchard culture, yet it is among the collection of nut trees, and from the native forests there are now to be had some very large, thin-shelled nuts of superior quality.

The Chestnut of sweetest flavor is the wild nut of the American forests. Selections of the largest and best of these are reported from many localities, of which not a few have been planted by amateurs. The larger nuts of Japan and Italy, having less flavor, are more in cultivation than the American varieties, yet when the American Chestnut shall have received the care and culture which have been given some other nuts, it is safe to anticipate a corresponding hastening of maturity, and improvements of size, etc.

This nut may be best prepared for market by bathing in scalding water as soon as gathered, and thoroughly drying till all surplus moisture is gone, so that moulding is avoided. The method is to place say a bushel of nuts in an ordinary wash tub and on these pour water boiling hot, in quantity sufficient to just cover the nuts an inch or two; the wormy nuts will float on the surface and are removed; in about ten or fifteen minutes the water will have cooled enough to allow the nuts to be removed by the hands; at this stage of the process the good of scalding has been accomplished (the eggs and larva of all insects have been destroyed, and the condition of the "meat" of the nut has been so changed that it will not become flinty hard in the further curing for winter use. Yet in this condition the nut is in no wise a "boiled Chestnut.") The water is drained off and the nuts being placed in sacks, in such quantity as will allow their loose spreading at about two inches thick, the sacks are frequently turned and shaken up as they lay spread in the sun or dry house. When surplus moisture is driven off, so that risk of moulding is avoided, the nuts may be packed in barrels or otherwise stored for winter. It will be found that such nuts are quite tender, retaining for a long period much of the qualities that make them so acceptable in the fall. Of course, nuts that have been scalded will not germinate.

Nuts that have been selected for planting, and no nuts of any kind should be planted that have not been selected for superiority of size, flavor or thinness of shell, are best cared for by planting in the fall in boxes of soil; their conditions of depth in the soil, and moisture from mulch, etc., to be as close a pattern of nature in the forests as possible, the object of the box being to faciliate the record kept and to prevent mice and moles from disturbing the nuts till the tap root has started growth in the spring. These boxes of imbedded nuts are settled in some protected spot of earth where pigs, squirrels, chickens and the like cannot get at them. The ground within the box being about on a level with the ground within the sunken box, say about two inches below the top of the box. In the spring these nuts, then bursting open with the growing germ, are transplanted to the nursery row or spot of ground where it is intended the tree shall grow.

The Black Walnut is reported wild over a broader territory than any other nut. In the early history of the country the trees of this nut formed large forests, especially in Southern Michigan and on the south side of the Ohio river. Of especially thin-shelled or extra flavored nuts of this kind there are very few reports, yet there are some reports of nuts superior to the average. The peculiar flavor of the Black Walnut seems to be less popular than the flavors of other nuts, and in this perhaps may be sought the reason why this once-abundant nut has offered so few selections for general culture.

A cheap and efficient method of cleaning the "hull" from the nut is: having placed the nuts, after gathering, upon grass in the shade of some tree or building for about ten days, till the "hull" turns dark and softens, then run the nuts through an ordinary corn-sheller and pick, by hand, the nuts from among hulls torn off by the sheller; place the nuts on shed or screen to thoroughly dry, away from any chance for sand to become imbedded in the rough shell of the nut. Only when thoroughly dried in a cool atmosphere are these nuts best. When stored for winter either in bags or barrels they should be kept away from heated rooms else the oil of the nut will become rancid and unpalatable.

The Butternut is worthy of more attention than it has generally received. There is but one report received by the Pomologist of a superior nut of this kind; possibly other people may become interested to watch for what may be growing wild in their neighborhoods, and the future may find culture and care developing this nut for a broader market.

Aside from its value as a nut for the use of the confectioner or for winter cheer, it is capable of being wrought into very unique ornaments.

With a very fine saw, cut across the nut into sections of about a quarter of an inch thick and it will be found that each section will present two very perfect heart-shaped and two diamond-shaped figures, from which the operator removes the particle of "nut-meat." On fine sand paper the two sides of the section are brought to a high polish, and the hearts and diamonds may be filled with different colored wax and the whole again polished on a stone. A pin secured to the back will serve to attach it to the dress as an ornament of no mean pretentions, but cheap.

In curing this nut, care should be taken, as with the Black Walnut, that no sand gets into the rough shell; a grain of sand thus lodged in the curing is apt to find its way among the kernels under the teeth of some unfortunate eater.

Carelessness in this particular has played its part in keeping these nuts from deserved popularity.

The Hazel nuts present some very large thinner shelled specimens of good flavor. Culture would probably so improve these as to make of this a formidable competitor of the Filbert, which, so far as the reports show, has not been satisfactorily grown in this country.

Of the Chinque, the reports and specimens received indicate a field for observation and culture that we may expect to remain but little longer unoccupied.

These nuts are broadly scattered over the country, growing invariably, so far as the report shows, without cultivation; they are best cured for market the same as the Chestnut, of which they are a dwarf species.

The Pinon, or Pine nut of Northern California, is quite unknown to the people east of the Mississippi river. This nut is marktable in immense quantities in the cities of the Pacific, where it is popular.

The Beechnut is larger and sweeter in the North and East than in warmer Central or Southern States. It is popular, and in places fashionable on hotel tables.

NUT CULTURE.

By Correspondent to Green's Fruit Grower.

THE DEPARTMENT OF AGRICULTURE will soon issue a report on the wonderful progress of nut culture in the United States. It is an entirely new industry. Ten years ago nobody ever thought of such a thing as cultivating nuts in this country. It seemed natural that they should grow wild and not otherwise. At present nut trees of many kinds are being grown and grafted in nurseries. Orchards of them have been set out in several States, and there is every prospect that by the time another decade has passed nuts will be plentiful in the market of varieties as superior to those now eaten as cultivated fruits are ordinarily better than wild ones.

At the show of the National Pomological Association, in Washington, the other day, nothing excited so much attention as a plate containing four huge open chestnut burrs. In each burr were revealed three or four gigantic nuts, as big as the French "Marrons." They were in fact obtained by a Pennsylvania grower by a graft of the imported Marron Chestnut on a native tree. In Japan grow the largest Chestnuts in the world. They are twice as big as the Marrons. Seeds of them have been brought to this country and propagated very successfully. Unfortunately, neither the Japanese nut nor the Marron is equal in quality to the Chestnut of the United States; but it is believed that eventually Chestnuts can be obtained by crossing the strains which will have the size of the Japanese and the flavor of the American. It is all a matter of grafting, and the nurserymen are pursuing the object in view most anxiously. There are already a number of growers in Pennsylvania, Delaware and New Jersey, who have orchards of trees in bearing.

How much can be accomplished by introducing foreign strains of Chestnuts no one can tell as yet, but there are native varieties which afford promises sufficiently certain and flattering. Some of these, found in Tennessee, Pennsylvania and the mountains of Virginia, are nearly as big as horse chestnuts, and have a most delicious flavor. Grafts from the trees bearing them produce admirable results. It must be understood that grafts do not improve varieties, merely maintaining them, so that the planter is able to gradually better his stock by selecting those trees which bring forth the best fruit. Perhaps the time may arrive when Chestnuts will contribute importantly to the food supply of the United States, as they do now in Europe. There are many ways of using them in cookery, and a number of recipes will be included in the government report above referred to. They are made into soup, prepared as a pudding, employed as a stuffing for birds, boiled and dipped in syrup for a conserve and utilized in several other fashions. Now and then a Chestnut twig is found which has a succession of burrs all along it instead of the usual two or three that dangle together. The Department of Agriculture would be very much obliged to any one who will send to it such a freak. It means simply that all of the female blossoms along the "spike" that bears the burrs have been fertilized by the pollen. Ordinarily only two or three of them are so fertilized. If some grafts of the unusual growth described can be secured, possibly the producing power of Chestnut trees may be multiplied.

Much is also being done in the cultivation of Hickory nuts. Nurserymen are planting and grafting the young trees, which they sell to growers. No orchards are as yet in bearing, but there are wild groves of fine varieties in Ohio, which are regularly harvested. There are Shagbarks in Iowa, of large size, which have such thin shells that they can readily be cracked by grasping two together in the hand. From such stock, grafts are taken by the growers, and the process of progressive selection will doubtless develop some very remarkable results in the course of a few years. Stories have reached the division of pomology of Hickory nuts in the Wabash valley as big as one's two fists. Much anxiety was felt to secure some of them, but it was finally learned that this estimate of size included the husks, the kernels being small and almost worthless.

Ohio is a remarkable State for nuts. A new kind of Black Walnut has been discovered out there, which is probably destined to be highly prized in the future. By a freak of nature one-half of its shell is not developed, nor the kernel on that side, the result being a pear-shaped nut filled with a single meat somewhat the shape of a peanut, though bigger. The important objection to ordinary Black Walnuts is that they are divided in the middle by a wall or shell so constructed that it is almost impossible to get the kernel out whole. This freak variety has only to be cracked to yield the meat entire. It is to be cultivated and may be expected to appear on the market by the time the present generation of babies is grown up.

A new and very extraordinary species of Hazel nut has been discovered in the State of Washington. Instead of being the fruit of a dwarf tree not six feet high, it grows upon a giant tree sixty feet in height. However, because the tree stem is only six inches in diameter, it cannot stand upright. Instead, it bends over not far from the ground, touches the earth, rises again, comes down to the ground once more, and so on for several snaky curves. Its branches bear Hazel nuts by twins. In every pod two nuts are found instead of the usual one. This is a variety well worth cultivating, and experiments are already being made with grafts from it.

Incidentally to this beginning of nut cultivation, varieties are being distinguished and designated by name. A few years hence one will not look in the market merely for Chestnuts or Hickory nuts, but for certain choice kinds. Already no less than fifty varieties of Pecans have been named. Of these last many plantations are in bearing and hundreds more have been set out in the Gulf States. Their stock has been obtained by grafts from wild trees in Texas and Mississippi, the fruit of which is paper-shelled, so as to be readily cracked between the fingers, and five or six times as big as ordinary pecans.

Great success is being made with the cultivation of English Walnuts in California. It is believed that they can be produced profitably in the Eastern States as soon as more experience is had in the fertilizing of the flowers. This is always a great difficulty, and it has been found on the Pacific coast that a very effective remedy for it is to plant among the trees Black Walnuts, or even the common Butternuts. They are all cousins and the plentiful pollen of the Butternut or Black Walnut trees fertilizes the blossoms of the English Walnuts, which would not otherwise be impregnated. Before very long this country will be shipping English Walnuts abroad, and the same is likely to be the case with Almonds. Of the latter very big crops are now produced in California and Arizona.

A BAG OF NUTS, WHENCE THEY COME.

TIMELY TALK ON THE NUT-PRODUCING TREES IN MANY LANDS—NUTTING PARTY IN ENGLAND—A REVERIE OVER THE WALNUTS AND FILBERTS, BRAZIL NUTS AND PEANUTS CALLS UP SCENES OF MANY LANDS AND STRANGE PEOPLES.

By Robert Blight.

"I have a venturesome fairy that shall seek
The squirrel's hoard and fetch thee new nuts."
—MIDSUMMER NIGHT'S DREAM.

THIS is the season of nuts, for they are ripening fast. The hurry and bustle of modern life have knocked all the nonsense out of romance, and one rarely hears of a nutting party now. We buy our nuts in the streets, so many "for five cents;" we do not gather them in "the merrie greenwood." As we go down the street we doubtless have a greater choice than if we strolled through the bosky dells, for here are Chestnuts and Walnuts (English and Domestic), Filberts, Cob-nuts and Barcelonas; Brazil nuts and Cocoanuts.

Give me, however, a good old-fashioned nutting party in the golden October days, when the woodland defies the artist with the splendor of its coloring. The merry laugh of the maiden and the youth, the gentle politeness of the youth as he holds down the bough and the coy acceptance of the maiden, as she picks the spoils; the affected fright as the fingers are impaled on the chestnut's spiny casing and the more than half-in-earnest solicitude as search is made for the thorn; the dainty way in which the walnut is picked up, lest its bruised rind should stain the "lily-white hand"—all go to make up a "vision of peace and plenty." But, like some other days, my nutting days are over, and as I sit in the study chair I view the nuts from the naturalist's standpoint, and leave to aldermanic and other civic dignitaries the privilege of lingering over the " nuts and the wine."

Nut-Producing Trees Hazel nuts, with which the nutting of England is mostly associated, are not so commonly eaten on this side of the Atlantic. In England the cultivation of Filberts and Cob-nuts is an important branch of horticulture. Both the European and American Hazel nuts are produced by trees of the genus corylus, belonging to the oak family. Filberts are elongated and have the involucere completely covering the nut. The name which attaches itself to a street in so many of the Pennsylvania towns is derived from the proper name Philibert, after a German saint of that name, whose day is August 22. The Cob-nut is rounder and less concealed by the involucere and grows in large clusters. The wild Hazel nut of America is smaller and has a thicker shell than the English nut. Barcelona nuts are only the fruit of the same tree as the English-Corylus Avellana, but, being grown in a warmer climate, have a thinner shell and a fuller kernel. They are very good eating.

The Spanish or sweet Chestnut tree, which supplies the Chestnuts roasting on the brazier at the street corner, is very nearly allied to the hazel tree, the oak tree and the walnut tree. Its botanical name is *Castanea Vesca*, and Gray looks upon the American tree only as a variety. It is a native of the countries bordering on the Mediterranean, and supplies no inconsiderable part of the food of the poorer inhabitants of Spain, Italy, Switzerland and Germany. The kernels are not only roasted, but ground into meal, which is used for thickening soup and for bread. The "Spanish" tree has been introduced into this country, and flourishes, but while its nuts are larger than those of the American form, they are not so sweet. The wood of the Spanish Chestnut is valued almost, if not quite, as highly as that of the oak. Many ancient wood-carvings have been executed in it, and it is very difficult to tell the difference.

The largest known specimen of *Castanea Vesea* in the whole world stands on the slopes of Mt. Etna and is called "The Chestnut of a Hundred Horses." A hundred years ago when measured it had a circumference of one hundred and ninety feet. We must not confound with this Chestnut the Horse Chestnut, which is grown as an ornamental tree for the sake of its beautiful foliage and spikes of white or scarlet flowers. It is very nearly allied to the maples. Its handsome, glossy nut, contained in a case which is rather warty than prickly, has gained for it the name of "buck-eye." Its kernel is unwholesome, but contains a large amount of starch.

Walnuts and Peanuts In the Walnuts we have a family kindred to the oaks, and natives of the temperate regions of the old and new worlds, affording like the oaks an interesting illustration of the fact that similar environments may produce similar forms. They are usually trees of large size, and supply valuable timber as well as palatable nuts. The species best known as supplying the "English" or imported nuts is the "Royal" Walnut, known as the common or English Walnut. It is a native of Greece, Armenia, Afghanistan, the Northwest Himalayas and Japan. Its nut is well known and appreciated for its thin shell, fine inner skin and abundant kernel. The young fruit is largely used whole for pickling. None of the native American species produce nuts of an equally excellent nature, for the folds of the nut are too woody and too complicated to let the kernel fall out of the shell. It has to be laboriously picked out, while the English Walnut easily falls out in two hemispheres. Hickory nuts, especially the delicious Pecan nut, and the Shellbark or Shagbark, are first cousins, we may say, of the Walnuts. Both Walnuts and Hickory nuts abound in oil.

What is that which crackles under our feet as we enter the theatre, the concert hall or the stairway to a political gathering? It is the Peanut. Verily, it reminds one of the parched peas of the Roman amphitheatre of the days of Horace and Juvenal, when the "gods" applauded or condemned in the intervals between the mouthfuls of their favorite esculent. Not that a Peanut is a bad thing, but a five-cent bag of them is rather out of place in the theatre, hall or church. It has several names—Earth-nut, Monkey-nut, Groundnut, Peanut, Manilla-nut; yet it is not a nut at all, botanically, but a pod of a leguminous plant called *Arachis hypogea*. These pods, which are stalked, oblong and cylindrical, and about an inch in length, containing one or two irregularly ovoid seeds, are produced underground. After the flower withers, the stalk of the seed-vessel has the peculiarity of lengthening and bending down, forcing the young pod beneath the surface, where the seeds are matured. A Clover, called subterranean trefoil, has a like habit.

The use of the Peanut must date back for centuries. In 1596 it was largely eaten on the banks of the River Maranon, in Brazil. Botanists are undecided as to its native country, some assigning it to Africa, others to America. In nearly all tropical and sub-tropical countries it is used at the present day, not merely for eating, but as a source of oil, of which the seeds yield a large quantity. It is of excellent quality and is a good substitute for olive oil in all its uses, although a little more liable to become rancid.

Curious Brazil Nuts The curious three-cornered, tasty Brazil nuts are the seeds of a remarkable tree called *Bertholletia excelsa*, belonging to the myrtle order. It attains an immense height, being sometimes one hundred feet before a branch spreads forth. These trees are curiously buttressed in the lower part of the trunk, the space between the buttresses sometimes accommodating half-a-dozen persons. Mr. Bates, the naturalist of the Amazon river, says that he saw many twenty or twenty-five feet in girth where they became cylindrical. Von Martins records some fifty or sixty feet at the same point. Mr. Bates writes thus: "The total height of these trees, stem and crown together, may be estimated at from one hundred and eighty to two hundred feet; where one of them stands, the vast dome of foliage rises above the other forest trees as a domed cathedral does above the other buildings of a city." The nuts are produced in large wooden capsules, containing eighteen to twenty-five of the nuts, which, falling to the ground, are gathered by the natives. When fresh gathered they are very palatable and are largely eaten. They also supply an excellent oil highly valued for cooking and by watchmakers. It is estimated that from Para alone some fifty million of nuts are annually exported.

In the same forests is found a kindred tree called the cannon-ball tree (*Lecythis Ollaria*), which produces similar nuts in an urn-shaped receptacle, closed by a lid and called by the natives "monkey pots." These nuts sometimes find their way into the market. They are very like the Brazil nuts, of a rich amber-brown color, with a smooth shell wrinkled longitudinally. Their flavor resembles the almond, and they would doubtless be offered for sale more frequently if they could be gathered like the Brazil nuts, but when the receptacle strikes the ground the lid falls off, the nuts are scattered and are eagerly seized upon by the monkeys and other wild animals.

Betel Chewing No book of travels in the East omits reference to the Betel-chewing habits of the people. It is said that one-tenth of the human race are addicted to it, men and women alike. The Betel-nut, called also Areca-nut, is produced by a palm, the Betel-leaf, used also in the mastication, comes from a vine allied to that which supplies black pepper. The Areca palm is common throughout the East Indian region, and is a tall, graceful tree. Its fruit is about the size of a hen's egg, and inside the fibrous rind is the seed called a nut, the albumen of which presents a mottled gray and brown appearance. When ripe it is turned into minor ornaments, such as buttons and beads. For chewing it is gathered before it is ripe, stripped of the husks, boiled in water, cut into slices and dried in the sun. It is then of a brownish-black color.

The way to chew it is to take a small piece, place it in a betel-leaf with a small lump of shell-lime, and, if you like, a small quantity of cardamous, or some other aromatic herb. The mastication causes a copious flow of dark-red saliva, which runs down the face in a way better imagined than described. The habit blackens the teeth, but, like all habits, it has its defenders, who aver that it strengthens the gums, sweetens the breath and stimulates digestion.

Materials for chewing in a siri-box are offered at all ceremonials as rigidly as the pipe of peace was at an Indian pow-wow. If two intimate friends meet, out comes the siri-box, just as the snuff-box was offered not so very long ago. Catechu, one of the best astringents in the *materia medica*, is obtained from the unripe nut by boiling.

Jamaica rejoices in the Bread nut, the fruit of a lofty tree. The nut is about an inch in diameter and contains a single seed, which when roasted or boiled is a very acceptable article of food. Fruiterers call the Butternut of Demerara the "Suwarrow" nut, as if the name was a corruption of that of the great Russian general of the end of the last century, who was so much admired by the Empress Catharine. It ought to be "Souari" or "Surahwa." It is the fruit of a forest tree which grows eighty feet high and is worthy of notice, for by persons qualified to judge it is said to be the finest of all the fruits called nuts. Few, however, are imported, and it seems to be a pity, for "the kernel is large, soft and even sweeter than the almond, which it somewhat resembles in taste."

The nut is about the size of an egg, somewhat kidney-shaped, of a rich reddish-brown color, and covered with large rounded tubercles. My own experience indorses the opinion given above and I have frequently regretted the absence of this delicacy from the market.

In tropical America the natives are blessed with a source of butterfat almost equal to that obtained from the cow. It is the Peka nut, obtained from a tree belonging to the genus which supplies the butternut of Demerara.

From tropical Africa there has been introduced into the West Indies and South America an important nut called the Kola nut. It contains in a very remarkable degree the stimulating principle of tea—theine—and that of cocoa —theo—bromine, besides other food constituents. Its value, therefore, to the inhabitants of a country where it grows can be readily imagined, and in Central Africa it forms quite an important article of commerce.

PROPAGATION.

IT IS CLAIMED by many that there is no more certainty in the reproduction of any variety of nut from seed than there is from an apple or peach, though the variation in some species is so slight that, in the absence of budded or grafted trees, orchards of selected seedlings are planted, with the possibility of getting many desirable nuts, though not of the exact type of the parent.

The difficulty with which some species are propagated by budding or grafting renders them so expensive that it is almost impracticable to procure an orchard of distinct varieties; therefore, notwithstanding the uncertainty of the seedlings, probably the most economical plan with such as Walnuts, Shellbarks and Pecans, would be to select the most desirable seed for planting, which should possess superiority in size, flavor, thinness of shell, vigor and productiveness of tree.

Germination The seed may be planted in the Fall, as soon as possible after they are perfectly ripe. Contrary to a prevalent belief, it is not necessary for them to become frozen in the seed beds, as many of our hard shelled nuts are natives of regions where freezing is unknown and many of our Northern nuts drop with or before the foliage of the trees which bear them, and in the still air of the forests or groves the snow lies level, while the dead leaves, with the snow, constitute a perfectly frost-proof covering, under which they will remain in good condition for years. They will germinate more quickly, however, if not allowed to become dry.

For most nuts select a high, well drained position and bury in heaps of sand. First, excavate the ground, which should be loose and porous, to four to six inches, then place a layer of nuts, then a layer of sand, then a layer of nuts, and so on until the stock is all stored; sprinkle with water and cover with six inches of sand and leave all undisturbed until Spring.

Should there be danger of mice or squirrels carrying away the nuts, place them in boxes, having first bored holes in bottom for drainage; cover top with wire netting and plunge in ground—or they may be set in cellar, and occasionally moistened, otherwise the sand will become dry and absorb the moisture from the nuts. It is also a good plan to mix a quantity of ashes with the sand in the box to prevent damage from ants, which may infest the kernels as soon as the shells begin to open.

Upon the approach of warm weather the beds should be examined, and after the kernels begin to swell the shells will open and the nuts should be taken out and planted about eight inches apart in drills four feet apart and covered about two to three inches deep and kept thoroughly cultivated the early part of the season; by late cultivation the growth will continue too late, the wood be immature and liable to winter-kill.

Root Pruning After making one season's growth in the Nursery, the root system may be much improved by pruning, as many species have only deep running tap roots, with but few, if any, fibers or lateral branches.

In order to root prune such plants, have the earth carefully removed from one side of the row so as to expose the tap root without disturbing it; take a sharp spade, push it below the exposed part of the tap root, severing it, fill up the excavation and tread it firmly. From this point of severance will be thrown out lateral roots, which will be of great benefit in transplanting.

Orchard Planting Budding or grafting is the method generally employed to propagate any variety and can be done either in the nursery row, and after having made one or two years' growth, removed to the orchard; or, the seedling trees first transplanted to orchard and there grafted. As the new varieties are high priced it is a good plan to set the orchard with seedlings and buy one or two each of the desired varieties to furnish grafting wood with which to top-work the seedlings.

Transplanting In transplanting the seedlings great care should be exercised to prevent exposure to the sun or drying winds. A damp cloudy day should be selected for the purpose, or they should be sprinkled with water and covered with a blanket while out of the ground, as a very little drying of the small fibers is more or less injurious.

Care of Trees and Plants on arrival from nursery If not ready to plant on day of arrival, or if you have more than you can plant within a few hours, they should at once be heeled in. Select a well-drained spot, dig a trench about eighteen inches deep, sloping on one side; place the roots in the bottom of the trench with the tops leaning up the sloping side. Spread out the trees so that the earth will come in contact with each and every root; then sift in fine dirt among the roots; fill the trench partly full, and press firmly with the feet; then fill up level with the top of the ground and press again with the feet and cover with loose dirt. Trees thus "heeled in" will keep in good condition a long time. Do not cover with litter or straw, as it will make harbor for mice during winter.

If frozen when received, bury the package, *unopened*, in well-drained ground, or place in a cool cellar so that it will thaw out slowly and gradually without being exposed to the air.

If they should appear dry or shriveled when received, through delay in transit or any other cause, take them from the package and plunge into a tub of water, or bury the roots in the ground in an inclining position, so as to cover one-half or more of the tops with the earth, and thoroughly soak with water and let it remain for twenty-four hours or more until they regain their fresh, plump appearance, when they may be planted.

Planting Dig the holes wide enough to admit the roots in their natural position, without cramping, and deep enough to allow the tree to stand the same depth it stood in the nursery; throw the surface and subsoil in separate piles; cut off smoothly from the underside all broken or bruised roots and cut back the past season's growth of top one-half to two-thirds, leaving two or three good buds to each branch--except for Fall planting in cold climates, when it is best to defer top-pruning until Spring, just before the buds start. At all times keep the roots carefully protected from the sun and wind. Place the tree in the hole; fill in with fine surface soil, working it in and among the roots, placing them out in their natural position; when hole is half full, pour in a little water and press firmly with the foot, filling all cavities and air space with earth so that it will come in contact with all the roots; continue to fill up and keep pressed until the hole is full, when it should be covered with loose dirt to prevent baking, *being careful not to get too deep.*

Never put any manure in the holes. A little Bone Dust or good rich soil is best in the bottom of the hole and the fertilizers applied to the surface and worked in. A covering of coarse manure, straw, litter, hay, or even stones the first season, will retain the moisture, prevent injury from drouth, and be of great benefit during dry season.

Nut Trees for Planting.

NUMBER REQUIRED TO THE ACRE, AND TIME REQUIRED TO COME TO FRUITING.

Distances for Fruiting.

	DISTANCE APART.	NO. PER ACRE.		TIME TO BEAR.
Chestnuts—American and Spanish,	40 feet,	28	Grafted,	3 to 5 years.
			Seedlings,	8 to 10 years.
Chestnuts—Japan,	25 feet,	70	Grafted,	1 to 2 years.
			Seedlings,	3 to 4 years.
Walnuts—Persian,	40 feet,	28	Seedlings,	6 to 8 years.
Walnuts—Japan,	30 feet,	50	Seedlings,	4 to 5 years.
Pecans, Shellbarks and Butternuts,	40 feet,	28	Seedlings,	6 to 10 years.
Almonds—Hard and Soft Shell,	16 feet,	170	Budded,	1 to 2 years.
Filberts and Chinquapins,	10 feet,	435	Seedlings,	2 to 3 years.

HOW TO PLANT.

USEFUL HINTS BY PRACTICAL ORCHARDISTS.

From The Farmer and Dealer.

PLOW DEEP that the roots may have a chance to grow, that they may have larger stores of plant food, retaining moisture and giving better drainage. The greatest precaution should be taken to protect the roots of the nursery stock, from the time it is taken up until transplanted. "A tree or plant out of ground is like a fish out of water; it is in a dying condition."

It is said that fully two-thirds of all the trees planted never reach the state of well developed, productive specimens. How necessary it becomes to perform each and every operation, from the planting of the seed to the final planting of the tree, and, in fact, its after culture, with the utmost care and attention.

Laying out an Orchard

THE WARNER PLAN.—Though thousands of trees have been set in this country, many persons still adhere to the old method of digging the holes somewhere near where the trees ought to be set, and sighting for an indefinite length of time to try to get the trees out so they will not look as if the Evil One, or some other gentleman, had dropped them promiscuously.

They can be set very quickly and easily as follows:

First.—Ascertain the size of the field to be set. Suppose, for example, it is 485 feet long and 246 feet wide, and it be desired to set the trees in the regular order, and 20 feet apart each way. Dividing 485 by 20 leaves a remainder of 5, one-half of which is 2½. Then the trees may be set 2½ feet from the outside, along the sides of the field; or setting one row less, dividing 20 by 2, and adding the quotient to 2½ feet, makes 12½ as the distance from the outside rows to the outside of the field. Or, they may be set 22½ feet from the outside along the sides. Dividing 246 by 20, and dividing the remainder by 2, the quotient is 3. Then the outside rows along the ends may be 3, 13 or 23 feet from the outside.

In setting a triangular field, or any other that is not rectangular, the foregoing is not applicable. In such cases the distance to be left outside of the outside trees can be determined only by the size and shape of each particular piece to be set.

Now, for a rectangular field, stake off a base line along one side or end, and set stakes at every twenty feet, or any other distance, if the trees are to be set more or less than twenty feet apart. Suppose stakes be set along the line A B of the rectangle A B C D.

Let A and B be the extremities of the row measured as the base line. It sometimes happens that there are fences or other obstructions in the direction of e and f, so it is not so easy to lay off a right angle from A or B as from some other point, as G. The surveyor's method of laying off a right angle with the chain along is a good way to lay off a right angle at G. To illustrate, take a rope, say seventy feet long. Measure off from G towards B, a distance $G\,h$, less than half the length of the rope. From G towards A an equal distance $G\,i$ equal to $G\,h$. Now, fasten the ends of the rope at the points i and h, or have two persons hold the ends at these points; carry the center of the rope out as far as it will reach in the direction of the line $C\,D$; set a stake, as at n,

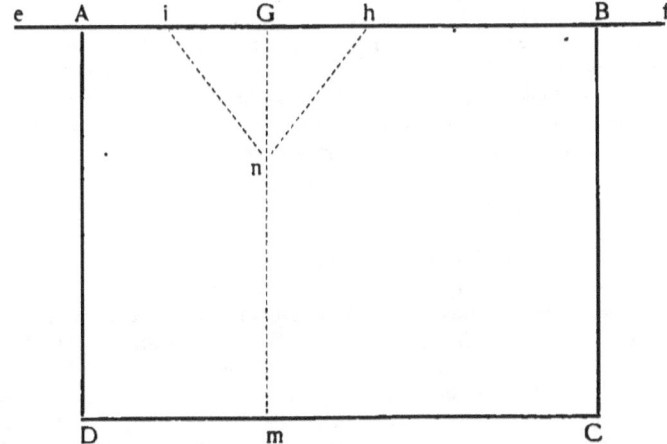

set a stake at m, in range with $G\,n$, and $G\,m$ will be at right angles to $A\,B$. It is necessary to be very particular in measuring from G to i and h, and in finding the point n. Set stakes the required distance apart along $G\,m$, measuring from G towards m. Now, measure off the required distance from m towards D, set a stake, and between this point and a point the required distance to the left of G, on the line $A B$, set stakes as on $G m$, measuring from the line $A B$. There will then be two stakes on the side $C D$, and using these as guides, the remainder of the line $C D$ may be staked. It will be safer, however, to measure from the base line $A B$ towards $C D$ for each row, as the stakes along $C D$ are liable to be an inch or a few inches out of the places they ought to occupy.

Having staked all the ground in this manner, take a board about four feet long and four inches wide, with notches as in the following diagram:

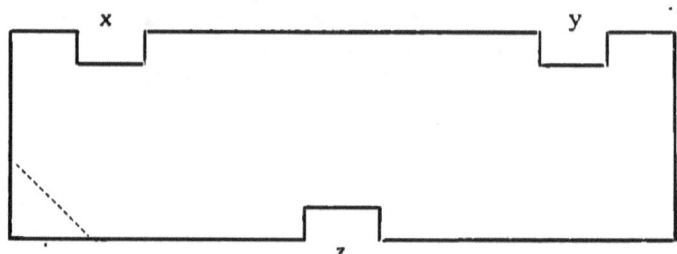

Be careful to have the notches x and y at equal distances from z, or cut off one corner of the board, as represented by the dotted line, and then be sure to put the same end of the board forward every time, both when completing the staking and when setting the trees. Put the board on the same side, every time of the stakes that mark the places for the trees; that is, not on the west of one, the east of another, etc. Having placed the notch z at one of the stakes already set, set stakes at x and y. When the stakes at z shall have been removed and the hole dug for the tree, the stakes at x and y should remain; then when the board is put to these stakes, in the same position it occupied when they were set, the notch z will mark the exact place for the tree. It is not absolutely necessary to mark all of the ground before digging part of the holes and setting some of the trees.

Inch redwood boards may be cut into pieces about a foot long, and split up for stakes, or even the thin redwood boards used as a lengthy substitute for shingles may be sawed into three pieces of equal length, and split up. Laths are very good for outside stakes; yet only a few of them are really necessary.

Persons who are very particular sometimes stretch a rope, as between the points G and m, and measure along the rope. The measure should be a straight pole, as long as the distance the trees are to be set apart.

The foregoing does not apply so well to very uneven ground as to ground nearly level; or rather, it is more difficult to apply these principles to very uneven ground, as it is more difficult to survey hills and mountains than to survey a level plain.

DONOVAN'S QUINCUNX PLAN.—With your permission I will briefly describe my method of laying out an orchard, which I have found to work well. I prefer the quincunx order in planting, as that method enables us to plant the largest possible number of trees on any given area, having the trees all the same distance apart. Each tree, by my method, is exactly the same distance from six other trees, as shown in the following plat:

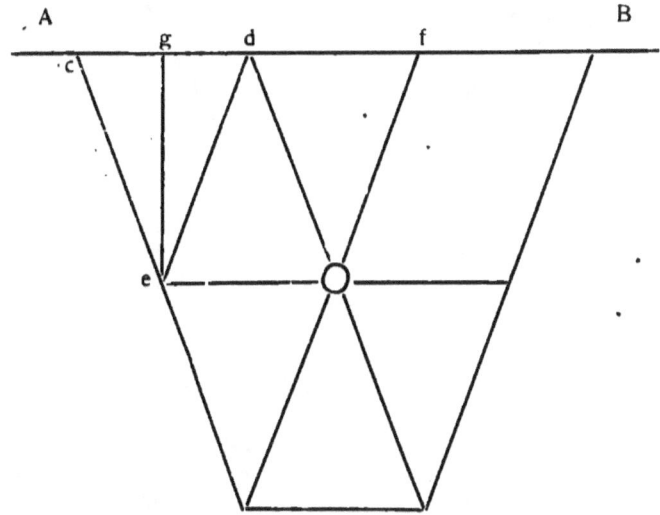

The tree at *o* is equidistant from six others, instead of four, and of course by extending the plat, each and every tree would be the centre of a circle of six trees.

Now as to the laying out. I take three strips of sheeting or batting, three inches wide, and twenty-four feet long (for apples,) make a triangle, each side being twenty-four feet; have the strips overrun about six inches, so that the ends will project three inches and form a notch, as per illustration.

I fasten the strips with a pin or bolt. With one man to help carry the triangle, and a boy to carry an armful of small stakes, we proceed to work. Commencing on the base line at *A* in the diagram we lay the triangle on the line *A B*, being careful to place the first stakes *c* and *d* true to the base line; a stake is placed at *e*, then we move the triangle forward and set another stake at *f* and at *o*; if care is taken to keep the base line perfectly straight the *stake* will be true on the next line, and you can go over a large area in a day in that

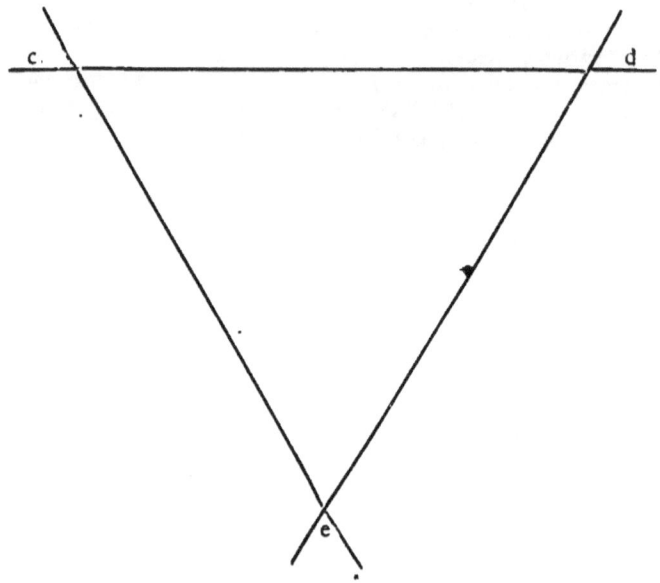

manner, setting two stakes at every move of the triangle. Then in digging the holes for the trees I use a triangle made of lath and shaped like the larger one. Place it on the ground so that the notch at *c* is against the stake; then stick a short stake in the other two corners *d* and *e*, and proceed to the next one. The use of the smaller triangle is the same as Mr. Warner's notched board. It enables us to set the trees exactly where the stakes were set, and thus insure a better looking job than if the trees were set hap-hazard. If twenty or eighteen feet is the distance required, the twenty-four feet triangle can be reduced to the proper size. By its use the stakes are set rapidly, and far more accurately than by any other method I have ever tried. If the ground is smooth and level, and the first line set accurately, the result will be satisfactory.

Strips of board will not shrink nor stretch like rope, and I believe will give better satisfaction than the looped wire plan. This triangle can also be used to determine the exact right angle from the base line *A B*. From the point *g*, half way between *c* and *d*, to *e*, describes an exact right angle to the line *A B;* but in the quincunx order of planting no attention is paid to right angles.

BUDDING AND GRAFTING.

BUDDING.

AFTER THE TREES are set in orchard the ground should be thoroughly cultivated. It may be planted to some hoed crop, but not to grass or grain, and after one season in orchard they should be grafted or budded to the desired variety, if not done before removing from nursery rows.

Budding   Budding is the operation of inserting the bud of a plant into or under the bark of another tree, for the purpose of raising, upon any stock, a variety different from that of the stock.

CUTTING OUT SHIELD BUD.   SHIELD BUD TIED IN STOCK.

Shield Budding   In Shield Budding the bud is inserted under the bark of the stock and is the method generally adopted, but with few exceptions has not proven successful with nut trees, other than the Almonds.

Flute or Annular Budding

Flute or Annular Budding is often successful when the ordinary shield budding fails. It is thus described by Prof. I. L. Budd, of the Iowa Experiment Station: "Top-working the Hickory or Walnut, or any common tree or shrub, can be done by annular (flute) budding. June, when the bark slips easily, is the time. Take scions one-fourth to three-fourths of an inch in diameter; remove a ring of bark one and one-half inches to two inches long, bearing a good, strong bud; cut off a limb of the stock, leaving a stub, from which another similar ring of bark is removed. The ring from the scion is carefully split if necessary and substituted, taking care that it fits, neatly, the remaining bark of the stub and that its edges, when split, are close enough to unite; cover the whole with a paper sack tied below the wound and success is sure. Care is necessary that the parts to be united fit and are not bruised." This method, as with ordinary shield budding, requires that the bud should be carefully wrapped with soft yarn, raffia or other flexible material to hold it in place and protect it from the weather.

GRAFTING.

Grafting

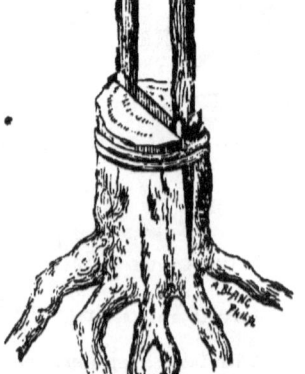

Grafting is the operation of inserting a scion or shoot into another tree and produce a growth similar to that of the scion.

There are many styles of grafting, but those generally adopted for nut trees are the Whip, Cleft and Bark Grafting.

Whip or Tongue Grafting

Whip or Tongue Grafting is the mode generally employed in root grafting or upon small stocks one-fourth to three-fourths inch in diameter. Scion and stock should correspond as nearly as possible in size. Make long diagonal cut across each; then cut each vertically so that the tongue of scion can be forced into the cleft of the stock, being careful that the line of separation

CROWN GRAFT.

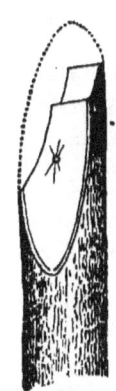  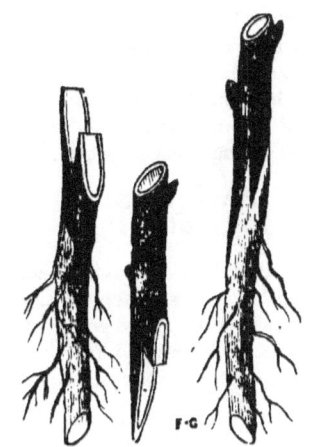

STOCK PREPARED FOR TONGUE GRAFT.   **TOUNGE GRAFT INSERTED.**   **WHIP OR TONGUE GRAFT.**

between the bark and wood of the one will fit that of the other on at least one side. They are now bound firmly by a bandage wound around them and waxed over to protect from the weather. During the season they should be examined, and as they enlarge the bands should be cut to prevent girdling the stock.

Cleft Grafting This method is generally used in top grafting and crown grafting. The stock is cut off squarely and split, and into the split a wedge-shaped scion is inserted.

The stock must be cut off squarely and smoothly with a sharp, fine-toothed saw, and the rough edges dressed off with a sharp knife, so as to insure a better union of scion and stock. The stub is then split to a depth of one or two inches, not exactly down the centre, but a little to one side is preferred. The scion is now

CLEFT GRAFT.

cut, in wedge form, with one edge a little thicker than the other and with but one scarf through the pith if possible. The blade of the grafting knife* is now removed and wedge at end inserted in cleft to open it for reception of scion, which is now pressed down to the first bud, the thickest edge of

*Grafting knife can be secured from seedsmen.

scion being on the outside. The line of separation between the bark and wood in the scion must fit that of the stock as in tongue grafting. To insure a union it is best to set the scions a little obliquely, the tops leaning from each other. The wound is now completely covered with grafting wax, not omitting the top of scion, unless it is a terminal bud, so as to avoid the exposure of any broken or cut surface, by which the sap can evaporate or the weather penetrate.

Bark or Slip Grafting This style is best suited to large trees, and cannot be performed until after the sap is running freely. The bark of the stock is merely cut through about an inch in length, after having been cut off as for cleft grafting, and if large may be so cut in several places so as to receive several scions. The scion is shaved from one side only, the point inserted in the slit under the bark of the stock and pressed downward, forcing it in until it becomes firm, when it should be tightly bound with muslin or wrapping yarn and all thoroughly waxed.

Care of Grafts The wood intended for grafting should have been cut and stored in ice house or other cool place while yet dormant; in cold climates where liable to be injured by winter, they should be cut soon after losing their leaves in the Fall and before freezing weather, and should be set as soon as the buds of the stock begin to swell, except for Bark Grafting, which cannot be done until the sap is more active.

The scions being dormant, the shoot from the stock will start before the graft and must be removed or they will rob the grafts of support. This operation of removing suckers should be repeated, during the season, as often as they appear. The grafts will soon make a rapid growth and become so top heavy as to render them liable to be blown out by storms. To prevent this the tops of the grafts should be pinched off after making about two feet of growth, by which the upward growth will be checked, the union strengthened, the growth become stockier and better able to resist the storms. For greater safety support the grafts by binding a stake to the stock and tying to top of graft.

Grafting Wax.

As given by the United States Department of Agriculture.

One pound linseed oil or tallow; six pounds resin; one pound beeswax. Melt all together.

Pour the mass into a tub or bucket of water to cool, thoroughly work it and knead it into balls of suitable size to handle. It is very important that all the ingredients be pure.

Liquid Grafting Wax.

By U. S. Department of Agriculture.

The following Liquid Wax is one of the best in use. It is ready at all times of the year to cover the wounds on trees and it is very serviceable in grafting. Applied with a varnish brush, the work is quickly and thoroughly done.

Melt one pound of common resin over a gentle fire, let it cool a little, then stir into it a tablespoonful of spirits of turpentine and seven ounces of ninety-five per cent. alcohol. If the alcohol cools the mass very rapidly it may be necessary to put it on the fire once more, stirring constantly. The utmost care must be used to prevent the alcohol from igniting. To avoid danger, remove the vessel from the fire when the lumps that have formed begin to melt. This must be repeated until the whole mass is converted into a homogeneous liquid like thick syrup.

ORCHARD CULTURE.

A FEW GENERAL REMARKS will be applicable to all species. Constant care, vigilance and culture are necessary for best results. The distances of planting will vary with different species, according to the sizes and habits of growth. To occupy the ground, in order to tide over the time from setting the trees till their fruiting, it may be planted to any cultivated crop, the fertilizing of which will at the same time nourish the trees until they attain a size that will so shade the ground that the intermediate crop will not succeed; after which the ground should be kept cultivated during the early part of the season and planted to some fall crop of rye, crimson clover or other green crop to be plowed under the following Spring.

As there is a great variation in the fruitfulness of individual trees of the same species of many nut-bearing trees, even under similar conditions, the question has arisen whether they are bisexual or self-fertile—that is, are the flowers of both sexes on the same tree. While probably the principal cause of failure is due to the different dates of blooming of the two sexes, or probably the unfavorable climatic conditions at time of blooming, and to guard against disappointment, we would suggest, as has been proven with some other fruits, for best results, not to plant too large a block of any one variety, but to plant, say, three to five rows of one variety, and three to five of another, and so on, so as to provide a continuous supply of pollen from those blooming at different times throughout the whole blooming period, and thus insure the pollination of the pistillate flowers.

All suckers should be kept rubbed off as they appear until the grafts become well established and heads formed, after which they will require but little pruning, except the suckers that will occasionally appear, and the adjustment of the branches so as to form a well balanced head.

As the nuts of different varieties ripen at different times of the season, as with fruit, it is well to consider this in setting the orchard, so as to have those ripening at same season planted near each other, to economize time in gathering the crop.

Contrary to the general belief, frost is not necessary to the ripening of the nut; nor in all cases to the opening of the burr of the Chestnut, as some of the early sorts, such as ALPHA, are generally open and gone three to four weeks before frost appears.

The frost will check the growth of the tree and circulation of the sap. The evaporation of the sap in the burr will commence on the outside exposed surface, which will rapidly dry and shrink, while the inner surface next the nuts remains moist, which will cause the burs to open and let the nuts fall out.

THE ALMOND.— (*Amygdalus.*)

ALMOND—HARD SHELL.

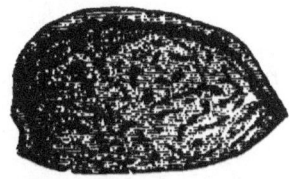

ALMOND—SOFT OR PAPER SHELL.

The Almond and Peach are considered to belong to the same species, and the wild Almond tree is probably the parent from which all the cultivated Peaches and Nectarines have descended. Of the early history and origin of the Almond very little is known, although it is thought to be a native of the mountainous regions of Asia, from whence it was taken to Italy, thence through France to Great Britain, where it was never grown to any great extent, but its cultivation confined to the Mediterranean countries, where it found a congenial home.

The European varieties were brought to this country and introduced in California in the early settlement of the State, though with very indifferent success, and not until after planting seedlings and much experimenting with new and improved varieties was the industry made profitable. It is claimed the Almond will grow wherever the Peach will thrive. This may be true with the tree, though they have failed to produce fruit at a profit in the Eastern Peach districts.

Many sections of the Pacific slope, as well as some of our Southern and Southwestern States, are thought to be suitable for the successful culture of the

Almond. It will thrive and bear fairly good crops on a poor, dry soil, but when given a rich loam and a liberal supply of water, on a well drained soil, it will give much better results. The European varieties are being superseded by native seedlings, which seem to have more vigor and productiveness.

In California the higher lands in the coast valleys and foothill regions are recommended as the best locations. They should not be planted where there is danger of late frosts in the Spring, as the trees bloom very early and the fruit buds are liable to injury, for which reason they do not succeed in the Peach growing districts of the Atlantic States. The important features of the nut are to hull easily, have clean, thin, soft shells and a smooth bright kernel.

They are used largely in confectionery, cooking, perfumery and medicine. The sweet variety forms a nutritious article of food. Of this variety there are three distinct types: The *paper shell*, *soft shell* and *hard shell*, the paper shell commanding best prices in market, the best varieties being sold to confectioners, the bitter variety being used in perfumery and flavoring.

Propagation of the Almond is mainly by Shield budding, as practiced with the Peach, on bitter Almond seedlings or Peach seedlings. Trees should be set in orchard at one year from bud and from sixteen to twenty-four feet apart, according to strength of ground, though probably the latter distance would generally be found best. At time of planting, the trees should be pruned to single stem and top taken off as with Peaches, though in after growth the branches should not be shortened in, as with the Peach, for the fruit is generally produced on the long slender branches or short fruit spurs in the centre of the tree. And after the tree comes to bearing very little pruning is necessary.

The Orchard should be thoroughly cultivated, but as the feeders run very close to surface of the ground, the culture should be shallow near to the trees to avoid injury to the roots.

The Almond comes to bearing at about three years from bud and increases with age until eight or ten years; an average of twenty to thirty pounds per tree is considered a good yield. The process of gathering and preparing the nuts for market is very simple. When the hulls are partly opened, disclosing the nuts, a large canvas is spread under the tree and the branches are whipped with poles until the nuts are shaken off. They are then run through a hulling machine and afterwards separated from the hulls by hand. The nuts are then bleached by sulphur fumes, to give them an attractive appearance. The longer they remain in the bleaching process the whiter they become.

The cost of gathering, hulling and bleaching Almonds amounts to about two cents per pound. The nuts sell at five to fifteen cents per pound, according to the variety. Some varieties, however, burst their hulls so nearly at one time as to need no bleaching, as they are not discolored by unequal exposure to the weather.

In preparing the nuts for bleaching, after they are separated from the hulls, they are spread out on trays and dried in the sun or dry house for a few days until they are dry enough to avoid moulding.

After thorough drying and bleaching, they are placed in coarse sacks and shipped to all parts of the world.

Insects and Diseases The almond being so closely allied to the Peach is liable to be attacked by the same insect pests and fungus diseases. The most troublesome of the insects are the *Red Spider* in California and the Peach Tree Borer, the former of which is readily destroyed by spraying in winter with a caustic solution for scale insects and a summer remedy recommended as follows: "Sulphur, three pounds; caustic soda, (ninety-eight per cent.) two pounds; whale oil soap, two pounds; solution in all, one hundred gallons. Directions: Boil the sulphur and caustic soda together in about two gallons of water. When the sulphur becomes dissolved, add the soap and boil until thoroughly dissolved; then add water to make in all one hundred gallons of solution and apply warm."

The moths of the *Peach Tree Borer* appear about June or July. The eggs are deposited on the stem of the tree near the surface of the ground, when they soon hatch, and the young bore through the tender bark and girdle the tree. Their presence is generally made known by the juices exuding and forming a gum on the surface.

As a remedy and prevention there should be thorough and clean cultivation and a careful examination of the trees in the Fall, and with a sharp pointed knife trace out and destroy every insect.

Tar paper and other protectors are sometimes bound around the butts of the trees in order to prevent a deposit of the eggs.

Of Diseases The *Shothole Fungus* has created the greatest injury. It attacks the foliage and young twigs. The first appearance is a yellowish brown spot on the leaf, which soon eats through the leaf and causes it to prematurely fall to the ground, thereby checking the growth of the tree, preventing the maturing of the fruit and formation of the vigorous fruit buds necessary for the next season's crop. The disease is thought to prevail to the greatest extent along the coast counties or sections most liable to heavy fogs.

As a preventive, Prof. Galloway suggests the application of ammoniacal solution of copper carbonate, as follows:

Copper carbonate,	5 ounces.
Aqua ammonia, (26 degrees,)	3 pints.
Water,	45 gallons.

The copper carbonate should be placed in an ordinary wooden pail and just enough water added to make a thick paste; then pour in the ammonia and stir until all the copper is dissolved. If three pints of ammonia is not enough to thoroughly dissolve all the copper, add a sufficient quantity to bring about this result. When completely dissolved pour the copper solution into a barrel holding forty to forty-five gallons; then fill the barrel with water. When ready to spray, take the concentrated fluid into the field, and for every three pints add forty-five gallons of water. The first application should be made as soon as the leaves appear, a second application in ten or twelve days, followed by a third two weeks later; six or seven applications during the season will be of benefit.

Varieties   There are a number of varieties being propagated and grown from the various seedlings that have proven profitable, and we suggest for each locality the best Seedlings that originated there. The catalogues name a long list, among the best of which are:

I. X. L.—"Large, broad, soft-shelled; kernel generally single, plump; nuts hull easily; tree upright, symmetrical with little pruning. Originated with A. T. Hatch."

King.—(King's Soft Shell.)—"Originated at San Jose. Shell very thin and soft. Regular and abundant bearer." *Wickson*.

Ne Plus Ultra.—"A paper shell; by A. T. Hatch; nut large and long; a heavy and regular bearer; it hulls freely."

BEECH.—(*Fagus.*)

The American Beech is abundant in the forests throughout a great portion of the United States, and its various sorts are largely planted for shade and ornament, though but little, if any, effort has been made to improve the varieties by seedlings, or propagate them for their nuts, though large quantities are produced by the natural growth and are considered valuable as an article of food for swine and poultry. The nut is small and resembles in outline a grain of buckwheat, and in flavor much like the hazel. With selection of largest and best varieties, under cultivation, the Beech nut might be so improved as to render their cultivation worthy of attention.

Propagation   The *Beech* may be propagated by the usual modes, viz: By seed, layers, budding and grafting, and thrive best in a cool, moist soil, and preferably in limestone regions.

THE CHESTNUT.—*Castanea.*

The Chestnut (European) is supposed to be a native of Asia Minor and derived its name *Castanea* from a city of that name, and from there was introduced into Southern Europe and disseminated throughout Greece, Italy, France, Spain and Great Britain. The *Japan* and *American* varieties are thought by some to be distinct species from the so-called European, though others claim them to be varieties of the same species.

The **American Chestnut** (*Castanea Americana*) is found in Southern Maine, Southern Vermont, New Hampshire, in Southern and Central New York, Province of Ontario, Canada, through Michigan and Indiana, continuing South through Kentucky, Tennessee and Mississippi and Northeastward throughout Georgia, Carolinas, West Virginia, Maryland, Delaware, Pennsylvania and New Jersey, finding most congenial soil and climate along the Blue Ridge and Alleghany Mountains and succeeding well at an altitude of three thousand feet.

It thrives best in high, dry, sandy, gravelly soil, well drained, with little or no limestone, though we have reports of fair success when planted in soil containing some limestone. While on prairie lands and rich river bottom soils it has met very little success, partially on account of its vigorous growth, immature wood and liability to winter kill. On the foothills of the Pacific slope it is also found to thrive and is being extensively planted.

In the Southern States we find another species known as the Chinquapin, (*Castanea Pumila,*) which is found to some extent in Southern New Jersey, Southern Pennsylvania and continuing on South and Southwest covering the Southern regions occupied by the American Chestnut.

The **American Chestnut** is a rapid growing, handsome tree, attaining very large proportions when standing alone with room for development. Leaves oblong, lanceolate and pointed, acute at the base, with coarsely dentate margin, smooth and green on both sides when mature. Branches long, slender and upright in growth. Burr small and opens in four sections. Nuts small, very sweet and delicate quality, with very thin skin. Hull generally covered to a large extent with fuz, in some cases very heavy, which feature gives them a stale, musty appearance, and is very objectionable to buyers. This, however, is partially removed by a process of rolling or scouring in barrels or in a sieve.

The **American Chestnut** makes a magnificent tree for lawn or roadside planting, and the young trees are valuable for stocks, on which to graft the improved varieties of European and Japan nuts, though some prefer the American seedlings of Spanish Chestnuts for this purpose, claiming greater vigor.

CHINQUAPIN.

Chinquapin, (*Castanea Pumila,*) is a smaller growing tree, sometimes attaining twenty to thirty feet; growth short jointed. Leaves smaller and narrower than the Chestnut. Burrs produced in racemes or clusters and containing one nut each. Nuts small, pointed, acorn shaped, with dark brown, mahogany colored shell; kernel very sweet and excellent. Burrs open in four sections. This nut is found in the Southern markets, but seldom reaches our northern cities. It ripens earlier than the American Chestnut, and with selected, improved varieties it should become worthy of cultivation.

Bush Chinquapin (*Castanea Nana.*)—A low growing shrub or bush attaining a height of eight to ten feet. General appearance much the same as the foregoing, though wood of shorter growth. Burr and nuts very similar, though the burr opens in two sections; found along the lower Atlantic Coast.

European Chestnut (*Castanea Vesca.*)—Trees large, stocky, heavy wooded, low headed, with broader spread in proportion to height; buds more prominent; leaves larger and thicker; burrs very large, with thick heavy husk, which is quite an objection, as, during rain storms, they absorb a great deal of water, and become very heavy, rendering them liable to break and mutilate the trees when bearing a full crop. Nut large and generally three to a burr; shell of nut thick and dark brown, with fuz around the point or stem; kernel is covered with thick skin, very bitter, and should be removed before eating; flesh coarse grained, dry and rich, though not so sweet as the American.

Japan Chestnut (*Castanea Japonica.*)—This is of moderate growth and as none are known to have come to maturity in this country we cannot state definitely their size, though in Japan they rarely exceed fifty feet. They appear to thrive in the lower New England and the Middle States and all down the chestnut region of the coast to middle Florida, where they make a luxuriant growth, and at this writing, February 1st, are retaining last years foliage, rank and green, which they will cast upon forming new growths, making it practically an evergreen tree. It is not thought it will endure as great a degree of cold as the American Chestnut. They are of long slender growth, with small buds, closely set and on opposite sides of the branch, though not exactly opposite each other. Leaves long and narrow, much like Peach leaves, finely serrate, indentations shallow, pale green above and lighter underneath. Burrs small, with very thin husk and short spines. Nuts very large, usually three to a burr, though sometimes five to seven. Shell thin, of light brown color, very smooth and entirely free from fuz. Skin thin and bitter. Kernel rather fine grained and sweet,

A TREATISE ON NUT CULTURE. 53

The **Japan Chestnut** comes to bearing very young, seedling trees generally at three to four years of age, and grafted trees at two years from graft, while the **Reliance**, a variety remarkable for its precocity and great productiveness, frequently produces nuts the same year the grafts are set.

Another valuable feature of the Japan chestnut is its early ripening, most varieties coming off before frost and two to three weeks in advance of the Americans, which gives them an advantage in the market. The past season the first shipments of Japan Chestnuts to New York market returned $14.00 per bushel; the next week $10.00, and the week following, after the European and American varieties began to appear, the price fell-to $8.00 and $6.00 per bushel, while the Americans were bringing $3.00 to $4.00 per bushel.

Prof. W. A. Buckhout says, in Bulletin of Pennsylvania Agricultural Experiment Station: "In the diversification of industries, which is now deservedly attracting so much thought and attention, the increase of our plants for cultivation should find a place, and of cultivated plants the nut-producing trees are among the most promising. Nuts have a higher nutritive value generally than have those fruits which are made up of the fleshy coverings of the seeds, as in the apple and peach, &c. They are rather of the nature of staple articles of diet, and approach the grains in food value. They are, moreover, not of the perishable class, and are easily handled with little waste and risk. While all the nut trees are probably capable of improvement, and each has adaptation to its particular sitution, the one most promising for Pennsylvania is the Chestnut."

In Southern Europe their food value is thoroughly appreciated, and it enters largely into their daily diet.

Paris alone annually consumes fifteen million pounds of Chestnuts. In Italy the peasant family that owns even one large Chestnut tree is sure of a living. If they want bread, the nuts are peeled and ground fine, and the flour they make is as white as prepared from wheat by the American "patent" process. If they want vegetables of any kind, the Chestnuts are boiled, baked with meats, roasted or made into soups. The Italian. cook books are replete with recipes for preparing Chestnuts.

For persons who cannot eat starchy foods, Chestnut bread would be more wholesome than wheat, corn or rye bread, since all the cereal foods are full of starch.

Americans have not an idea of the economic value of the Chestnut tree. We are as ignorant as well of the value of most of the other nut-bearing trees.

FOOD VALUE OF CHESTNUTS.

From the Christian Register.

When the cereals cease to be cultivated, the "granaries of the world" will no longer be the vast plains of Australia, India, Russia and the Western States of America. They will be the now untilled hillsides of the temperate zones, the now impenetrable jungles of the tropics. The mountainous regions of our Eastern States will regain the agricultural supremacy of the country. The trackless wilds of Africa, South and Central America will be the greatest agricultural regions of the world.

Of the plants growing in the temperate zone, there is but one which will become a substitute for the cereals. Where a wheat field produces from fifteen to twenty-five bushels an acre, a Chestnut grove on the same area will produce over and over again that amount of equally nutritious food. The Chestnut grove requires no cultivation. The late frosts of Spring and the drouths of Summer will not materially injure the crop where wheat crops would be ruined. The fortunate owner of a Chestnut grove can gather his nuts in the Fall, and the rest of the year he can labor at whatever task he chooses. In all the countries of Southern Europe, Chestnut flour is largely consumed, and the demand exceeds the supply. Bread, cakes, pies are made from the flour, and the nuts also boiled and eaten whole. The European nut is much larger than the American variety, grows on a larger tree, and is much more prolific. It will flourish here, as has been proved by trial, and the larger Chestnut, which must be cooked to be palatable, is now found in most of our markets.

If Chestnut flour is such an excellent substitute for wheaten flour, and is so easily and cheaply produced, why do we not find more people cultivating Chestnut trees? The Chestnut tree requires a long time to come to a bearing age, though it continues to bear for centuries. The man who would plant a Chestnut grove to-day would leave a rich legacy for his grandchildren, but would himself receive little return for his expenditure. Few men wish to lose the use of any considerable part of their land, in order that their posterity may have a rich inheritance. Even in thickly populated European countries no one plants a Chestnut grove. The groves are all of natural growth. The farmer desires the present use of his land, and will not alienate it for the sake of posterity. When once the Governments actively interest themselves in the food problem of the future, Chestnut trees will be set out on Government lands; year by year small tracts of farm lands will be planted by their proprietors, and in the course of a few generations Chestnut groves will abound. In our country, where the various State Governments foster tree planting, where there is an annual arbor day, why should not the trees planted be trees which, as beautiful and long-lived as any trees that grow, at the same time would contribute to the national food supply? If the State Governments of New England and the middle Atlantic States desire to preserve the water powers of their rivers by returning the shorn hills to forests once more, let them plant Chestnut trees. If the States of the West desire to prevent disastrous floods in the great rivers by establishing timber reservations on the higher lands, let them plant Chestnut trees. If village communities desire to beautify the drives of their vicinity by planting trees along the roadside, let them plant Chestnut trees.

The above remarks have reference to the NATURAL growth of Chestnut, while the *grafted varieties come to bearing earlier*, are *more productive* and *valuable*.

The Chestnut tree, on account of its magnificent proportions, handsome form, clean, healthy foliage and freedom from insect enemies, is admirably adapted to ornamenting large grounds or roadside planting. The prevalent idea that they are a long time in coming to bearing is entirely removed since the practice of *top grafting* with the *improved* varieties has been more generally adopted. Many sorts of recent introduction, when grafted in American Chestnuts, will produce nuts at *second* or *third year* from graft and some of the Japan sorts the year the scions are set.

The American Chestnut in its natural form in open ground attains immense proportions. In the town of Mansfield, Conn., on land of Mr. Whipple Green, stands a giant, whose circumference at four feet from the ground is twenty-three feet. It is heavily buttressed all around, and the trunk is apparently sound. Four large branches have been sent out; the lowest, ten feet from the ground, measures sixteen feet four inches in circumference. The circumference of the buttresses at the ground is fifty-four feet. The diameter of the spread of the branches is eighty-three feet from northeast to southwest, and from the northwest to southeast one hundred feet. In height it is estimated to be eighty feet.

In Sicily, near Aetna, is reported an immense Chestnut tree that measured one hundred and twenty feet in circumference, whose shade could shelter one hundred horses and whose hollow trunk admitted two wagons side by side.

CHESTNUT CULTURE.

In his remarks on this subject before the New Jersey State Horticultural Society, at their recent meeting, Mr. Charles Parry, among other things, said:

"At the present prices of these nuts there is no more inviting field in all horticulture than the growing of Chestnuts. At this time, when the prices of many farm products are verging on the cost of production, and some going far below it, Chestnuts alone not only yield a large profit to the grower, but sometimes make returns that seem fabulous. This, too, with large tracts of land, suitable for growing this crop, to be had for from $5 to $10 per acre.

"It seems strange that the United States cannot supply itself with Chestnuts, a crop so easily grown that once planted the tree continues to grow and yield annually for centuries. Yet such is the fact. Every year, after exhausting its own supply, the United States draws upon Southern Europe for large quantities, and yet the land in Southern Europe available for the Chestnut is but a small percentage of that suitable for it here. When we compare the standard price of Chestnuts in this country, from $4 to $8 per bushel, and remember that Chestnuts can be produced cheaper than wheat, we see at once the enormous margin of profit in favor of Chestnuts. When we further reflect that any enterprising grower can secure from $6 to $10 per bushel for a large part of his nuts, we are able to appreciate the profitable nature of the crop.

"The reasons for this state of affairs are several. One is the long time, judging from the common American Chestnut, that it would require for a Chestnut Orchard to come into bearing; another, that comparatively few farmers are acquainted with the improved varieties of Grafted Chestnuts, and it is only these that are worthy of being cultivated; still another, that many farms are worked by renters, and these would not be likely to plant orchards of Chestnuts. These causes will continue to be operative for many years to come, and it is for this reason that Chestnut growing is such an attractive field for the enterprising horticulturist. For many years in the future it must remain a pursuit of large profit and with little competition. Individual trees frequently yield from $30 to $50 each, and yields of over $100 per tree are on record from trees standing alone. An orchard could not be expected to average more than one-quarter of these amounts. A planter, however, can reasonably expect an average yield of over a bushel per tree, or about $200 per acre, and this with but very little expense for either care or fertilizers.

"In planting a Chestnut Orchard, care must be taken in selecting the site. It is more particular in this respect than either the apple or the pear. Wet land, even if underdrained, is not suitable. Neither is dry land, with a compact, impervious, clay sub-soil. The Chestnut loves a loose soil, with a deep, open, porous sub-soil, and if this porous sub-soil is fifteen to twenty inches deep it will be all the better.

"In setting out an orchard of Chestnuts the trees should be about forty feet apart, and in the center between four Chestnuts place an Apple tree, and between Apples and Chestnuts two Pear trees or Plum trees of upright growth. By this means a larger return from the ground will be had at first, and, as the Chestnuts need the room, the other trees can be cut away. Any crop that is cultivated and fertilized may be grown among the trees as long as it will pay. An orchard planted in this way will pay its way from the start; in five years the trees will begin to make handsome returns, and in ten years should yield from $200 to $300 per acre annually.

"Now, as to varieties. There is as much care needed in planting a Chestnut Orchard as an apple or pear orchard. An orchard of seedling Chestnuts is just as worthless as an orchard of seedling apples or pears, no matter how large the nuts may have been from which the seedlings grew. None but grafted trees are worth considering. There are two other requisites as important as size, and these are earliness and productiveness.

"To secure large prices the nuts must be early; to secure large returns the trees must be productive. No matter if a nut is large and early both, if it does not load the wagons it will not yield large returns. Quality is of little account. I never saw a Chestnut buyer taste a nut; appearance is of more account. A light colored, bright nut, free from fuz, of medium size, four or five inches in circumference, sells best in the Philadelphia market. In planting an orchard a succession of varieties is desirable, so as not to have the whole crop on hand at once. The following will make a good succession of profitable varieties, ripening in the order named:

"First. Alpha, the earliest Chestnut, a good grower and bearer; nuts about four inches around; brought this Fall 40 cents per quart or over $12 per bushel.

"Second. Advance, ripening about five days later; a good grower and bearer, large in size; brought this Fall 30 cents per quart, or over $9 per bushel.

"Third. Reliance, ripening four or five days later; not so fast a grower as the preceding, owing to its enormous loads of nuts, which are large, smooth and handsome; brought this Fall 25 cents per quart, or about $8 per bushel.

"Fourth. Giant, ripening four or five days later; good grower and nuts very large, six inches around; not so productive as the preceding.

"Fifth. Paragon, ripens later and is of better quality than any of the preceding. It is large and productive, and brought this year 20 cents per quart, or over $6 per bushel.

"The above varieties are enough for any commercial orchard, but there are several others of merit that can be included where a larger list is desired, viz.: Success, Numbo, Ridgely, Scott, Hannum, Miller and others. Any of the above varieties will commence to bear in two years from planting and increase yearly in their yield.

"Some of these varieties are much more liable than others to be infested by worms. Scott is remarkably free from these pests. Others, especially the early varieties, are very liable to attack.

"There seems to be but one way to combat this enemy, and this is to gather daily all fallen Chestnuts, destroy the wormy ones and treat the rest with bi-sulphide of carbon. By this means the number of beetles will be greatly diminished. Where there are large groves of wild Chestnuts near-by that are not attended to, even this plan will be only partially successful.

"There are two ways of obtaining a Chestnut grove—namely, by grafting a natural grove or by planting arable land. In grafting, the best time to commence is after the timber has been cut two years. The sprouts have then grown to a proper size and the best results will be attained at this age."

FRUIT NOTES FROM WOODBANKS.—THE CHESTNUT CROP.

T. Griener, in American Gardening.

In earlier issues of *American Gardening* I have repeatedly told of the two-acre Paragon Chestnut orchard, which we planted in 1893 in Ontario county. The results are already beginning to show. Although the wood-growth has not been remarkable in amount for the past three years, the trees being still quite small, yet it has been healthy and the little trees this year have given us all the fruit that they could hold up. It was a sight, indeed, to see these little trees with branches bending low under their load of the remarkably large and heavy burrs. Many of the latter contained four and five nuts of the largest size, larger than we have seen them elsewhere, and especially on the trees at Woodbanks with its apparently ailing foliage.

It is evident, however, that we have made a mistake. The Paragon tree seems to be bound to fruit almost from the start. We should not allow it to indulge in this wasteful inclination. The few quarts or baskets of nuts that we can get from the trees during their first three or four years, or even the few bushels to be harvested for some years more, cannot possibly compensate for the loss in wood-growth. Fruit production requires considerable energy. We want the trees to exert all their efforts in healthy wood-growth, in order to come to full bearing size at as early an age as possible. The comparatively few nuts which the trees gave us this year cannot help but reduce the bearing wood one-half for another year, and the nuts of the next crop, if allowed to remain on the trees, must necessarily again largely reduce the bearing wood for another year, perhaps one-half or more.

It will be an interesting experiment to watch the development of trees, some of which are allowed to fruit while others have every effort at fruit production literally nipped in the bud. This experiment we propose to make. Only a few of the trees will be allowed to fruit for years to come, but we feel even now quite sure of the outcome—so sure that I would advise every one who has a Paragon tree to remove the burrs as soon as set every year for at least ten years, with the exception perhaps of leaving a very few nuts to ripen for the sole purpose of satisfying the grower's curiosity.

On the whole, I am now more enthusiastic than ever about the possibilities of growing Chestnuts for pleasure and profit when we have such an excellent nut as the Paragon. The only drawback seems to be the difficulty of getting an orchard started. Even with the greatest care in planting and caring for them, an undue proportion of the trees die during the first or second year, and have to be replaced. Even now, after repeated efforts to get the vacancies filled in, there are a number of trees missing, while there is not a vacancy among the Japanese plums planted alternately between the chestnuts in each direction.

There is one point on which we need more light—namely, the union of stock and graft. Many of our trees show a considerable enlargement of the stem above the union, evidently the Paragon portion growing more rapidly than the native seedling stock. The question is, whether the union is perfect or not. Sometimes I fear that the union will always be a weak spot in the tree, and yet our Paragon at Woodbanks, which showed the enlargement from the start, is apparently outgrowing the difference, the stock gradually catching up with the grafted portion.

PARAGON CHESTNUT CULTURE.

By J. S. Woodward.

Acting on the advice of *The Rural New-Yorker*, in the Spring of 1890, I bought three Paragon Chestnut trees. They were planted in vacant places in a grove of common Chestnuts. Two lived, and I am ashamed to acknowledge that they have been utterly neglected, never having had any mulching or care beyond being let alone. Neither of them is over seven feet high or three-fourths of an inch in diameter of body, but this past summer one of them produced three burrs, each with three Chestnuts, and the other had seven burrs with three nuts in each burr. Here was this little tree with twenty-one nuts, each of the weight of four average nuts from the common trees. This would make the crop equal to eighty-four common nuts. The number of nuts was a surprise to me, and if the common trees in our grove had produced Chestnuts in proportion, we would have had more than five hundred bushels. I tested them in comparison with the common nuts, and gave them to others to taste; all agreed that they were equally good. I also showed them to a dealer in our city, and while the common nuts were selling for $5 per bushel, he said he would gladly pay $8 for such as these.

In the Spring of 1892, we sent a hired man into our Chestnut grove to cut down some other trees which were growing there. Through a misunderstanding of the order, he cut some forty Chestnuts before we discovered what he was doing. The trees cut varied from four to eight inches in diameter. To make the best of the situation, we let the sprouts grow about the stumps, as the quickest way to repair the damage. These sprouts made a growth of eight feet on an average and last spring I sent for scions of Paragon and Numbo, and grafted from three to five sprouts about each stump. I had the impression that it was very difficult to successfully graft the Chestnut and so I took great pains in doing the work. I selected scions and stocks as nearly of the same size as possible and used the splice or tongue system of grafting, winding well with waxed cloth. A part I grafted quite early and others after the leaves on the stocks were nearly as large as a mouse's ear, having kept the scions in the sawdust next the ice in the ice-house. To my surprise and great joy more than seventy-five per cent. of the scions grew, though some grew so rapidly that they were broken off by the wind before fully united. They have made a growth of from four to six feet and some have produced over twenty-five feet of new wood; all have ripened up as sound as a dollar. From present appearances —judging from what the two little trees have done, many of these scions will bear another year. Now, I am more than glad that our Dutchman did not better understand English. We shall have the rest of the natural grove cut down so as to graft the sprouts that spring from the stumps. As no insects ever attack the Chestnut here I believe a Paragon orchard will pay more money than the same land in apples.

PARAGON CHESTNUTS.

By J. S. Woodward.

ANOTHER YEAR'S EXPERIENCE.

Older readers may remember that a year ago I gave my experience with two trees of Paragon Chestnuts, and also the result of grafting the Paragon on common sweet Chestnuts. For the benefit of new readers, let me say that the two trees which we have were planted in the Spring of 1890, one year grafts, and that in the Summer of 1893, one of them bore seven burrs with three Chestnuts each, and the other three burrs with a like number. These trees are now about one and one-half inches in diameter of body, not over seven feet high, and with a spread of top of not over four feet. The one that bore twenty-one Chestnuts last year was more exposed than the other, and the late frost we had last Spring so killed the young growth that it bore no fruit this year. The other, bearing nine Chestnuts last year, started with twenty-two burrs this year, but being away from daily observation the Summer web-worm got upon it, and so ate the leaves from one limb that the burrs dropped from that, and it matured but seventeen burrs. But before they were fully ripe, some vanda stole the most of these, so that we got only sixteen Chestnuts this year. I weighed these and they averaged a little over one ounce to four Chestnuts.

Some of the grafts set in the Spring of 1893 bore nuts this year, and all have made a very strong, healthy growth, and show every indication of great fruitfulness next season. I last Spring grafted a lot more, and among others I cut off quite large trees and cleft-grafted them the same as I would the Apple. On others, I inserted scions in the side of the trunks, and these have made a good growth. Next Spring I shall cut the main body off just above the grafts.

I grafted some quite early, and others just as the buds were nicely swelling. I also put in other scions after the bark would start quite easily, and I came to the conclusion that if the scions were cut in proper season, and kept perfectly dormant, that it does not make much difference when the grafting is done. Only, of course, the scions cannot be inserted on the side of the trunk until the bark will start easily, as in this style of grafting the scion is cut slanting from one side to a point, and inserted under the bark similar to a bud in budding, but having the end sticking out a couple of buds.

A successful method of grafting is to cut off a limb or the main trunk, about an inch or so in diameter, and insert scions cut the same shape as those last mentioned, under the bark, waxing the whole end of the stub. Two or more scions may be inserted in a stub, but one is a plenty to let grow. In using this method, of course the bark must be loose. But don't make the mistake I did in several cases; don't shove the scion down so far that a little of the cut surface does not extend above the end of the stub, for if you do, no union can take place above the cut surface, and a bad job is the result. In all systems of grafting the Chestnut, I have found it to pay to use waxed cloth, and firmly bind the limb until growth takes place to such an extent that the band is liable to strangle the young growth.

I notice that a good deal is said about the Chestnut not making a good union of stock and scion. I have closely examined mine, and while occasionally one does not seem to be perfectly joined, the majority have made a good union, and on a good many it would puzzle one to find the place of grafting. I have had a few to break with the wind, but in no case has it been at the collar. Next Spring I intend to cut off and top-work a good many trees which I have that are from four to six inches in diameter of trunks. I will do this as I would an Apple Orchard, using the limbs and spreading the top as much as possible, so as to have them come quickly into fruitage. I have tried budding this past Fall, but so far have had no success. Will some one give needed instructions if "the thing can be did."

CULTIVATION OF THE CHESTNUT.

FACTS ABOUT GRAFTING THIS NUT.

From Rural New Yorker, 5, 19, '94.

Any Practical Future for the Business?

1. How high are your trees grafted? 2. Does the scion unite perfectly? 3. Have you known the top to blow off on account of weakness at the point of union? 4. At what size and age do your improved Chestnuts bear? 5. How many nuts to the burr? 6. How about size and quality compared with wild Chestnuts? 7. Do you think Chestnut culture promises any practical rewards to farmers or others?

How to Start the Graft.

By a Reader.

1. Five to six feet. 2. Not always on young trees. On large trees worked in branches from one to one and one-half inches thick, the scions take as readily and make as perfect a union as the Apple. In the nursery I have the best success in whip-grafting, having the scion and stock of equal size. 3. Yes; sometimes the scions will make a growth of two to three feet, and do not apparently form a particle of union with the stock. My opinion is that this occurs from too free a flow of sap. If the scions are cut before the sap begins to flow, and left to wither somewhat, they may be successfully grafted up to the middle of May, and the union will be more perfect. 4. They usually commence bearing the second year after grafting. I am alluding to the Paragon. The Numbo will take several years longer. The Japan I consider of very little account compared with the above varieties. Some of the Japan varieties bear very fine nuts, but they shrink much quicker than the Paragon and Numbo. 5. From one to four, sometimes five to six. 6. The size is generally from three to four times as large as the common Chestnut. In quality they are not as fine as the common Chestnut, but, like the Concord among Grapes, they are good enough for the masses of consumers; boiled or roasted they are excellent. 7. Emphatically, yes. If a young farmer would plant a grove of one thousand trees now, ten years hence he would have an independent competence.

Chestnuts or Apples for Profit.

By W. Atkinson.

1. I think about one foot high. 2. It does in the case of Numbo, perfectly; of my first trees of Paragon, apparently the union was not so perfect.

3. I have had no tops blow off. 4. At three years, they bear a few. 5. Usually three nuts to a burr. 6. The size is fully double the average native Chestnuts; quality less than half. 7. Only moderately so. I would rather expect to profit more from an Apple than a Chestnut Orchard.

Notes from a Big Grove.

By Joseph L. Lovett, Bucks County, Pa.

I have a grove of nearly one thousand Paragon Chestnut trees. 1. I generally graft my trees four to five feet from the ground. 2. The scion does not always unite perfectly on American stocks, but on Spanish there is in every case a perfect union. 3. In all my experience, I never had but one top blow off, and that happened when the tree was loaded with nuts; it broke at the union of the scion with the stock. 4. My Paragon trees commence to bear when four to five feet high; they bear the second year from the graft. The great trouble with me is that they bear too full every year. Paragon has no off years. 5. Generally three nuts to the burr; sometimes as high as five to seven to a burr. 6. The size is very large; forty selected nuts will make a quart, dry measure. They sell at forty cents a quart, or one cent apiece. When boiled, the quality is as good as the wild nuts. Paragon ripens from ten days to two weeks ahead of the common wild Chestnut; for that reason a better price can be had for them. 7. There is great promise in Chestnut culture for those who have the time, money and patience. But little attention has been given to it; the wild or American has become almost extinct in some sections. What will prevent extensive planting is the great difficulty of getting the trees to grow; some seasons from one-half to three-fourths will be lost by transplanting. Another great difficulty is the grafting, which will make the tree always sell at a high price.

A Profitable Business on Suitable Soil.

T. T. Lyon.

1. One, a Paragon, is grafted about two feet above the surface. Others, Japanese, at or beneath the surface. 2. The Paragon, grafted at two feet, does not form a satisfactory union; although other Paragons, Japanese and European varieties, seem to form satisfactory unions at or beneath the surface. 3. None of these, in my case, has been broken off, at the point of union, by wind or otherwise. 4. Two-year-old grafts have generally fruited at from one to three years from the date of planting. 5. Paragon has generally produced two or three nuts to the burr, while the number of burrs has sometimes been such that one-half was removed soon after setting. One of the most produc-

tive Japanese varieties produced a very heavy crop upon a tree less than six feet in height, each burr being even smaller than those of our wild natives; but invariably with a single large, round nut in each. 6. Paragon is nearly, though not quite equal in quality to our natives, and in size, fully the equal of the Europeans. The Japanese, above referred to, is of similar size and quality; but with a slight astringency, which disappears when dry enough for use. 7. It is my conviction that, with the Paragon, and, probably, with some of the Japanese varieties, a profitable orchard business may be conducted upon a suitable soil. This conviction is based upon a two or three years' experience in fruiting the Paragon, and but a single season's fruiting of the European and Japanese varieties.

Needs Careful Work to Propagate.

C. H., Conestoga, Pa.

My experience with Chestnut culture is with Paragon, an imported Japan, and the Italian. I have not found the last two profitable. The Japan is very large and fine looking, better in quality than the Italian, but not so good as the Paragon. It is not productive—many of the burrs are nutless. 1. It is important to have a strong stock, an inch or more in diameter, but for a good union the graft and stock should be of the same size; therefore we must set the graft two to four or six feet up. 2. Often defective. This is another reason for not grafting in the heavy stock near the ground. The wind would break it off sooner than the graft set on the pliable stock. 3. Yes, but so far not seriously. It sometimes makes unsightly knots; how these will behave when the trees become large remains to be seen. I had hoped to avoid these defects by root grafting, but my root grafting did not prove a success. Budding makes the best union, but this is also very uncertain. In fact, success in propagating Chestnuts does not by any means amount to one hundred per cent. 4. Usually the second year after grafting I have had from three to four quarts on four-year-old grafts worked in the top of a two-inch stock. 5. Generally three. 6. The average Paragon would probably weigh three to four times as much as the average wood Chestnut. In quality it is nearly as good. 7. I think it does. The trees bear young and abundantly, and rarely fail to make a crop. Rough land not adapted to general farming is suitable for a Chestnut orchard. Grafts set on young sprouts in the wood lot will be profitable in three years.

The Union Seems Perfect.
Isaac F. Tillinghast.

Our experience in Chestnut culture is not extended enough to prove of much value as yet, the trees having been set but three and four years. They were Numbo and Japan Giant, grafted four or five feet from the ground. The union between stock and scion seems perfect enough, as none has broken apart. Last season the trees averaged, perhaps, ten burrs; some had two and some three very large nuts in each, which ripened before our native nuts. We think the quality excellent, in fact, fully equal to small, native nuts. We see no reason why it would not be a profitable industry, and have seriously contemplated setting a large orchard.

Regrets for Small Planting.
C. Cooper, Pennsylvania.

I have had some experience, but only in a limited way, having but few trees bearing. One of these is about twenty-five years old, and for several years has annually produced from one to one and one-half bushels. Had I, when it was planted, put out ten or twelve acres, they would have long since paid for the ground, labor, interest, taxes on land, and been netting now a nice income, with no expense, except for gathering the crop. This tree is of the Spanish variety; the fruit is about two and one-half times larger than the common wild nut, and of equally good quality. 1. We graft from six inches to three feet above the surface, according to conditions. 2. The union seems to be good after the second year; occasionally by storms or accident, if the growth is strong, perhaps two or three per cent. may be broken. 3. I have never known them to break after the third year. 4. Generally the third or fourth year, when they would be, if grafted on a stock not removed, eight to ten feet high. 5. One to three nuts to the burr. 6. I have never found the quality of Paragon, Numbo or any of the very large nuts equal to that of our Spaisnh nut.

THE CHESTNUT IN CALIFORNIA.
By Felix Gillet, in Pacific Rural Press.

Last Spring, a very good book from the Department of Agriculture, entitled "Nut Culture in the United States," was issued, but on account of an act of Congress, passed last winter, limiting to an edition of one thousand copies all bulletins, reports, etc., containing more than one hundred pages, only one thousand copies of that book were published. The Department could not be blamed for such a niggardly edition, which, as the *Rural Press* remarked in its issue of May 16th, rendered it wholly inaccessible to the tens of thousands who would be interested in it. Congress alone was to blame for it. But to make up for the deficiency, the *Rural Press* published the principal portions of the book, those relating to the Walnut and Almond, as being of great interest to the people of this State. As you didn't give any extract from that portion of the book relating to Chestnuts, I would like to have you publish in your columns a short essay of mine on that very nut.

First, I would call your attention to a paragraph of the aforesaid book, page 80, under the heading of "Budding and Grafting," doing great injustice to that important member of the nut family, the Chestnut, as far as this State is concerned, and reading as follows: "Neither budding nor grafting is very successful with the Chestnut in the dry climate of California."

As I have budded and grafted with success on my own place, in Nevada City, for the last twenty-six years, thousands and thousands of Chestnuts, that extract greatly surprised me; so I remonstrated with the Department against such a sweeping assertion, telling them that they were doing a great injustice to our State in publishing such an erroneous statement, especially in a work of that kind, and assuring the Department that it had surely been imposed upon by some ignorant horticulturist.

Mr. S. B. Heiges, head pomologist of the Department, replied to me as follows:

Regarding your comment upon what is stated in the bulletin on "Nut Culture," page 80, concerning grafting or budding the Chestnut in the dry climate of California, I would state that you were the only party who reported success, and that there are portions of California in which the climate perhaps is much dryer than where you are located. From what I have been able to learn, your climate more closely resembles that of the Eastern States than any portion of California. Here, our successful Chestnut grafters consider anything less than ninety per cent. as a partial failure. Amongst others who have reported their experience in grafting and budding the Chestnut in California, I may mention Luther Burbank, who reports: "Neither budding nor grafting is very successful in this dry climate."

Thus it appears that Mr. Luther Burbank was the person who gave the Department such erroneous information. That Mr. Burbank met with failure in budding and grafting the Chestnut on his place in Sonoma county I will not dispute, though it greatly surprises me; but he should not have *generalized*, and more so when his information was to be published in that book, and assert that "neither budding nor grafting is very successful in the dry climate of California." But it is a fact that Californians are too apt, when failing to accomplish one thing or another, to throw the blame on our *dry* climate, but never on themselves. Now, let me tell you that such is not the case, for the

Chestnut can easily enough be budded or grafted in California, if we only know how to do it; and I assert that the climate either of Nevada or Sonoma counties has nothing whatever to do with the success or failure in budding and grafting the Chestnut, as one is certainly as dry as the other. I know positively that the summers in this county are terribly dry and hot. Now, for the benefit of the readers of the *Rural Press*, I will hereby describe how to bud and graft the Chestnut, giving them at the same time some general ideas on its culture and planting and the harvesting of its nuts, and figures showing how important has become in other countries the culture of that nut tree.

GRAFTING THE CHESTNUT.—If asked at what time of the year I graft the Chestnut, I would answer: At any time from March 1st to October 1st; for I have grafted (common cleft grafting) Chestnuts with good success in the Spring, also in midsummer (July) and in the Fall (from September 20th to October 1st.) For Summer grafting I used with equal success scions kept in sand in the cellar, or wood of the year's growth right from the tree. The reason why I practice Fall grafting—not only on Chestnuts, but also on Apples, Pears, Prunes, etc., and, as I tried for the first time this Fall, on Walnuts—is because I have more time and leisure to do it in the Fall than in the Spring, at which time work of all kinds crowds up all around on the place. Grafting done in the Fall keeps dormant, the same as budding, the grafts putting forth in the Spring at the same time as buds do. But the grafts must be taken from that part of the scions where the wood is perfectly round and not angular-like—that is, from the base of scions. I graft also one-year-old trees as large as a pencil, at the table, in February, planting them out in the Spring, succeeding forty to fifty per cent.; a larger number if the stock is of a larger size.

Chestnut grafting is as successful on large as on small trees. If a limb is too big it is better, as with the Walnut, to use sap grafting, which consists in making two clefts, one across the stub at each side of the center, right in sap wood, instead of making a single cleft through the center. In inserting the graft one must make allowance for the difference in thickness of bark of both stub and graft, and insert the graft so that the wood of the graft will unite with that of the stub.

BUDDING THE CHESTNUT.—Budding can as successfully be performed on the Chestnut as grafting; it may be done as early in the Summer as after July 4th, and the buds be made to grow to quite a length before the Fall; dormant budding, however, is preferable. It is done in August and September; but a condition *sine qua non* of success with the Chestnut, as with the Walnut, both stock and scion must be fully in sap; it is to say that Chestnut budding should rather be done late in Summer or early in the Fall. The same as for grafting, the wood of the scions from where the buds are taken should be perfectly round. The stock or shoot to be budded should be of the size of the fore and medium fingers. Shield, plate and ring budding are used on the Chestnut with about equal success; plate and ring budding, however, being much more liable to succeed than shield budding. In performing the latter operation the shield of bark from the scion should be cut two inches long and wide in proportion. Too small stock, which would be of very good size for Apple, Pear, Peach, etc., will not do to be budded. When the stock or shoot is of the size of the medium finger or thumb, or larger yet, I always use plate and ring budding. If the ring of bark taken from the scion goes only half way round the stock, it is what is called plate budding; if it reaches all around it, it is what is called ring budding; but in both cases it is the same principle, only that in plate budding so much of the bark is left on the stock, only enough being taken out to allow the insertion in its place of the ring of bark from the scion, generally smaller than the stock. Chestnut stock sometimes does not grow the first year large enough to be budded; in that case it is left over for the ensuing year, being cut back close to the ground in the Spring to make it grow a new shoot of the proper size; for the operation of budding is much more successful on wood of the year's growth than on two-year-old wood—exactly the same as with the Walnut, and don't you forget it.

SOIL AND EXPOSURE.—The Chestnut is a hardy tree whose crop, except that of the Japan Chestnut, is seldom injured by late frosts in the Spring. I never had any of my French varieties of Chestnuts injured on my place by frost at any time of the year, and, furthermore, they bear regularly and heavily every year. The Chestnut is a regular mountain tree, and may be regarded right at home in our mountains. The soil best suited to the Chestnut is a sandy, granitic, or ferruginous sandy-clayish, deep soil. In Nevada county, up to an altitude of three thousand feet, can be seen twenty-five-year-old French Chestnuts bearing well and bearing nice nuts. This nut tree is certainly better adapted to Central and Northern California than to the southern part of the State, and it is a fact that wherever the Olive does well the Chestnut does badly, for it is too hot for it. The Chestnut will mature its nuts well at an altitude of three thousand feet in the latitude of Northern California and at four thousand feet, probably, in the mountains of Southern California; but wherever Summers are either too short or too cold for the nuts to mature well, only such varieties as are known to mature their nuts in a shorter time should be planted, and there are such varieties of Chestnuts, though the nuts are smaller.

In mountain gorges and with a sunny exposure the Chestnut does splendidly, otherwise an eastern or northern exposure is best for the tree. In the red clay of our mountains, with a little mixture of decomposed granite, in soil so hard and impermeable that holes dug in it will hold water for weeks, the Chestnut does surprisingly well, and I have an idea that when planted way up in the mountains, say at an altitude of Nevada City or two thousand five hundred feet, the Chestnut is less particular on the nature of the soil, though, the same as with the Walnut, the richer and deeper the soil is the more thrifty will the Chestnut grow.

IRRIGATION.—In very dry soil a little water through the summer months will be of great benefit to Chestnuts, but too much water, I believe, would affect the nuts in this way, that it might retard their maturity. Several years ago, in irrigating nursery stock, I had a stream of water running constantly at the foot of a grapevine, and the grapes never matured on the vine, and this summer I had water running almost constantly at the foot of a Chestnut of the very kind maturing its nuts in a shorter time than other varieties and the nuts matured badly, while trees of the same kind in nursery rows, and very little irrigated, matured their nuts splendidly. It shows that intensive irrigation is as bad for nuts as it is for fruit and grapes. Fruit, for instance, will grow much larger if given plenty of water, but its keeping qualities will be destroyed and often injured. It is to say that if Chestnuts, like any other class of trees planted in dry soil, will be benefited by irrigation, too much of it might hurt. It would be wise to stop irrigating *bearing* Chestnut trees one month to six weeks before ripening time.

REPRODUCTION AND PLANTING.—The Chestnut does not reproduce itself very well from the seed, hence the reason why that tree is invariably grafted to obtain those large round nuts known the world over under the name of "Marrons," or French Chestnuts, the kind used as dessert, either roasted or boiled. The American Chestnut is propagated from seed, and is almost barren in California, but much better results would be obtained as to size and productiveness, if not quality also, if its best types were propagated by grafting, which I myself intend to do hereafter, having for that purpose procured, through the Department of Agriculture, at Washington, scions from two good bearing trees on a farm in old Virginia.

Chestnuts should be planted from thirty to thirty-five feet in rows, when planted in orchard—farther apart if it is desired to plant between the Chestnuts fruit trees bearing a crop sooner, such as Prunes, Apricots or Peaches; for Chestnuts, like Walnuts, require some time to bear a regular crop. Chestnuts do very well planted in clusters on hillsides, or in rows, alongside fences, but inside of them, or scattered all around, a few here and a few there, either in field, vineyard or orchard; but I would not plant any as shade trees on public thoroughfares, such as streets and roads, for the boys, and girls, too, will go after them in a lively way, throwing stones and sticks into the trees, to make the nuts drop down to the ground, to the great annoyance of the owners of the trees. I know some people in Nevada City who, to put a stop to the nuisance, had their trees cut down, entirely doing away with them.

In France, as with the Walnut, seedling trees are planted to create a

Chestnut Orchard, and grafted (cleft-grafting) or budded (ring-budding) at the top, five or six feet from the ground, when large enough to undergo the operation. Pruning the Chestnut is useless and even hurtful, the only pruning necessary being the cutting off of dead wood, or limbs in each other's way, or to give the top a nice shape, but the very top of the tree should be left alone. Fruiting wood forms itself naturally, no trouble about it, and is not helped out by pruning, as is the case with fruit trees, and besides, it lives a long time. When the trees are getting very old pruning is beneficial, for, by cutting back limbs worn out with age, it compels the tree to grow a new top. Here, under the hot sun of California, I find that it is better to train the tree rather low. This is the way I do it: First, I let the tree branch out at five or six feet, letting the lower limbs spread out to their full length—and Chestnuts have a great tendency to spread and especially on the sun's side—then I support with poles those lower limbs, never trimming them off, and making it high enough for any man to stand up under the tree; for it is those very limbs that bear the most of the nuts and the largest and finest ones; if those limbs were not propped up they would bend down to the ground under the weight of the heavy burrs, as such is the case with Marron Chestnuts.

HARVESTING AND PREPARATION OF CHESTNUTS.—The Chestnut at this altitude ripens its nuts from the middle of October to the first of November, the prickly burr cracking open at the head, showing the brown shell of the nuts inside, which drop to the ground when the burr is fully open or the wind shakes them down. However, to accelerate the harvesting of the nuts, and when the burrs have taken a dark yellow color which tells that the nuts inside are ripe, the burrs and nuts are knocked off the limbs by striking on the latter with long, flexible and slender poles. A little wooden mallet is generally used to open the burrs falling to the ground and which do not burst open naturally. Boys stealing nuts simply use their two feet in squeezing out the nuts from their prickly envelopes. The nuts are then placed in a shed to sweat—that is, to throw out their vegetation water—and shipped immediately to market, if to be used *fresh*.

In the island of Corsica, where Chestnut trees comprise one-third of the wooded part of the island, they first cut down in August the grass, ferns and briars that cover the ground under the great Chestnut trees, so as to permit the harvesting of the nuts with more ease. The harvesting of Chestnuts in that island lasts twenty-five days and is done by women, who are boarded, and at the end of the harvesting are paid, not in money but in "bleached Chestnuts," that is, twenty-five gallons of bleached Chestnuts for twenty-five days of labor. Bleached Chestnuts are Chestnuts dried hard and cleared of both hull and pelicle; in short, ready to be ground for the manufacturing of meal or flour, extensively used in all Chestnut-growing countries. Three gallons of fresh

Chestnuts are required to make one gallon of bleached Chestnuts. By the way, Chestnuts so dried keep a long time, and are packed either in sacks or hogsheads.

THE FOREIGN VARIETIES.—The common European Chestnut, whether French, Italian or Spanish, is small, flat on both sides—at least half of them—and grows generally four to eight in one burr. This is the kind that is dried hard and bleached for the making of meal and flour; bread, cake and a delicious mush, eaten with milk, being made with it. The cultivated Chestnut—the kind raised for dessert and market, and which is either roasted or boiled—is the Marron. It grows generally single or in pairs, sometimes three in one burr. Apropos, I could not but smile in going over some Eastern nursery catalogues to read about Chestnuts bearing as many as four to six nuts in a burr, the nurserymen laying a stress on so many nuts found in burrs. Well, that is a defect, if raising nuts for market, for the less nuts in the burr the larger and, consequently, the more marketable are the nuts, the same with Walnuts; kinds that bear large nuts may, for instance, yield less nuts per tree, though the same quantity in bushels or pounds. Anyway, as small nuts are almost unmarketable, or, at the best, held at very low prices, it is much more profitable to raise large nuts, which are always marketable and at fair prices. So it is with Chestnuts.

The **Marrons**, the largest Chestnuts raised, have a glossy shell, and, when roasted or boiled, the inner skin comes off nicely. If roasted, a small incision should be made with a knife at the small end, to prevent the nut from bursting open with a loud report; if boiled, the shell should be first removed and then boiled in water the same as potatoes. They are delicious cooked both ways. Our confectioners are now roasting them in their peanut roasters, and people seem to take well to them. A Thanksgiving turkey stuffed with chestnuts is getting to be quite *a la mode* up here in this Chestnut-growing region, and is a capital dish; and I predict that in a given time, when Marrons will be grown plentifully in California, as they should already be, every Thanksgiving turkey on this privileged coast will be stuffed with chestnuts.

IMPORTANCE OF THE CHESTNUT TRADE.—The Chestnut trade in France, Italy, Turkey and other countries of Southern Europe is simply immense. In Central France the Chestnut is called the "bread tree," and some years there is such an abundance of nuts that cattle are also fed with them. The average production of a grafted Chestnut or Marron in full bearing is estimated at sixty kilograms (one hundred and twelve American pounds.) I have a Marron Combale Chestnut tree on my place, planted in the Spring of 1871, which averages ninety pounds of nuts per year, for which I have refused fifteen cents per pound; last year that tree yielded one hundred pounds of nuts, but only seventy pounds this year, which decrease in yield was surely due to our exceptionally bad Spring, which killed all my fruit crop. I find Chestnut trees up here to bear regularly every year, and heavy crops, too. France makes an immense consumption of Chestnuts, and though the production within her own territory reaches enormous proportions, she has still to import large quantities of the nuts and meal from other countries. Italy has one million five hundred thousand acres planted in Chestnuts, producing five million eight hundred thousand quintals of Chestnuts (a quintal is one hundred pounds.) In 1880, that country exported to France twelve million pounds of Chestnuts and Marrons, valued at $350,000.00. In 1881, Turkey exported to France seven million two hundred and forty-six thousand quintals of Chestnuts, Marrons and Chestnut meal. In 1881 France exported over fifteen million pounds of Marrons, Chestnuts and meal, valued at $560,000.00; five million pounds going to England, the balance to Switzerland, Algeria, Germany, Holland and Belgium. Paris alone consumes twenty million pounds of Marrons (table or dessert Chestnuts) yearly. In the Department of Dordogne, and where such large quantities of Walnuts are grown, there are two hundred thousand acres planted in Chestnuts, this Department exporting $400,000.00 worth of Chestnuts of all sorts. In the Department of Ardeche, where the soil is of a granitic, volcanic formation, one hundred and fifty thousand acres are planted in Chestnuts; mostly Marrons or Chestnuts for market are raised in that Department, they selling for almost twice as much as common Chestnuts.

In the Island of Corsica the Chestnut is planted up to an altitude of four thousand feet. There are trees in that island measuring twenty-five feet in circumference and which are eighty feet high. And so on in many Departments, especially in Central, Eastern and Southern France. In the Department of Haute-Savoie, where there are immense quantities of Chestnuts, are several establishments manufacturing gallic acid, which is extracted from the wood of the Chestnut, and selling for $5.00 to $6.00 per two hundred and eleven pounds (one hundred kilograms.)

FUTURE OF THE CHESTNUT IN CALIFORNIA.—Thus we see of what immense importance is the growing of the Chestnut in France and Southern Europe, and the question that naturally occurs to our mind is: Why should not we, here in California, where half of the territory may be said to be well adapted to the culture of that tree, raise the Chestnut, at least the Marron Chestnut, on a large scale, and then add another important product to our already large list of products of all kinds? That Chestnut culture is possible if the trees are planted in those parts of our State well adapted to it, is sufficiently proved by trees found in the mountains and in full bearing. I have the pleasure of sending a box of Marron Chestnuts for you to sample, roasted and boiled, and I want you to tell if there is not in our great and privileged State quite a future for the production of such nuts.

NEVADA CITY, CAL., November 24th, 1896.

IMPROVED CHESTNUT CULTURE.

A NEW INDUSTRY—WASTE PLACES MADE GLAD.

From Rural New Yorker.

The *Rural New Yorker* has always stoutly contended that American agriculture, from the day the Pilgrims left the Mayflower, has been but a record of utilizing wastes. The first corn crops grown in New England were planted on worn-out soil, with a large fish in each hill for manure. From that day to the present, American farming, as it spread toward the West, has ever gone through the same performance; exhaust the land by continuous cropping and then either run away from it "out West," or make use of manurial substances that were previously regarded as useless wastes. Save the wastes or retreat! That has been the alternative, and this question of waste-saving has been so well studied and practiced that immigration to the West has been almost stopped, while to-day alert Eastern farmers on the old soil, that has given crops for more than a century and a half, have safely weathered the storm of business depression.

But how about the waste *land?* In every neighborhood—on almost every farm east of the Ohio River—there are rough and rocky hillsides, where, apparently, nothing but wood will grow. These places are usually held at a loss except as they furnish firewood or timber. It is doubtful if much of this timber-land will yield income enough to pay taxes—much less interest on the value at which the land is held. The object of these articles is to describe one of these rocky hillsides that has been cheaply utilized for a profitable crop. It is waste land turned to account. On the hillside, so steep, rocky and hard that a woodchuck could not burrow in it, I saw a crop growing that will in a few years yield as much money to the acre as a crop of potatoes. This crop requires neither plow, cultivator nor harrow—neither manure nor fertilizer—nothing but knife and brush-scythe. The crop is improved Chestnuts.

There is no fairy tale about this business. The hill, the trees and the man are all to be found any day. At Marietta, Pa., close to the east bank of the Susquehanna River, lives Mr. H. M. Engle, well-known to our readers as a good farmer and an expert in nut culture. On the east side of the river is a gently rolling country, stretching back for miles, and covered with beautiful farms. Directly opposite, on the west bank, steep hills shoot up almost directly from the water's edge. This ridge is thickly covered with timber—Chestnut predominating. The land has never been cultivated—nor can it ever be—with ordinary crops, being far too rocky and steep for horse or farm tools. It must ever remain in forest. As to the value of such land, Mr. Engle says that he bought some of it just before the war at $20 per acre. Now it could probably be bought for $12. On this hillside I found twenty acres of Paragon Chestnuts—grafted on sprouts from the stumps of natives, which were cut off for firewood, or posts and rails. None of these trees is over five years from the graft, yet with only the older ones in bearing the estimated yield this year is seventy-five bushels of nuts. To one who can actually see the trees and the way they are growing, the possibilities of this nut culture are very apparent.

For over fifteen years Mr. Engle has propagated and tested the Paragon Chestnut. The *Rural New Yorker* has already given the story of this nut, and described its behavior at the Rural Grounds. As to its size, the *Rural New Yorker* found that forty-two Paragon nuts weighed a pound, while two hundred and eight native American Chestnuts were needed to give the same weight. As to quality, while not so sweet and tender as the small natives, it has none of the coarse and bitter taste so objectionable in the Japan and Spanish varieties. We have always found it a very heavy bearer of large, handsome burrs. In fact, the *Rural New Yorker* from the first has been almost as enthusiastic as Mr. Engle over the possibilities of Chestnut culture.

Mr. Engle was quick to see the chances for profit in a good Paragon grove. Every year we import large quantities of Spanish nuts, even though no effort has been made to popularize the Chestnut as a cheap *food*—not as a luxury. If he could grow large quantities of the Paragon—a better nut in all respects than the Spanish—there seemed no good reason why they should not sell readily. Then the question arose, where should they be grown? Should he set out orchards on good lands suitable for vegetables or fruits? Mr. Engle is an "intensive" farmer. He grows now, on twenty-five acres, with the aid of green crops and fertilizers, a more valuable crop than he formerly grew on one hundred and twenty acres with the manure from thirty cows.

He could not afford the land for a Chestnut orchard, for his soil must yield crops at once. But there was that idle Chestnut ridge across the river. If it could grow wild Chestnuts, why should it not grow Paragons? If it is possible to graft a fine and valuable apple on the stock of a worthless variety, why would not the same hold true of Chestnuts? The result was that a small portion of the timber was cut off and sold. Paragon grafts were set on the sprouts, and these first grafts are the five-year-old trees of to-day.

CHESTNUT GRAFTING IN NEW ENGLAND.

By J. H. Hale, in Rural New Yorker.

Taking a day off last week, I visited the farm of Judge Andrew J. Coe, of Meriden, to look over his extensive operations in the grafting of Japan Chestnuts upon our native stock. As the *Rural New Yorker* has, I believe, been the foremost paper in America to advocate nut culture for profit, I thought possibly a few sample nuts, as well as a few notes, might be acceptable at this time, when so much attention is being given to this important and growing subject.

Mr. Coe has, for many years, been a firm believer in the profitableness of nut culture in New England, and has tested by grafting most of the European varieties and their seedlings that are now grown in this country. While he has had fair success, it was not until the advent of the Japan varieties that he was fully satisfied that in these we had something that would unite readily with our American stocks, and at the same time give us nuts of extra large size and of high quality. Being satisfied of this, but not fully satisfied as to the hardiness of the Japans, he, four years ago, grafted some on native seedlings in low land, where the frosts of early Fall and Winter were the most severe and dangerous. The growth has been marvelous, and grafts put into a three-inch stock, eight feet from the ground, four years ago, have now formed a strong, bushy head, fully ten feet across, and bore freely this season, after the last very severe winter, when Snyder Blackberries, the most hardy type we have in New England, were entirely killed to the ground in an adjoining field. This certainly tests the hardiness of the Japans.

Several years ago, Mr. Coe bought the choicest selection of Luther Burbank's ten thousand Japan seedlings, and it is not only the largest, but sweetest Chestnut I have ever seen. More recently he has bought two others of Mr. Burbank, and on the wooded hillsides, above the city of Meriden, has grafted an eighteen-acre block of native Chestnut sprouts with these improved Japan seedling nuts. .

My visit at this particular time was to study the effects of grafting at different seasons of the year. Both cleft and crown-grafting are practiced, mostly on stock one to two inches in diameter, four feet from the ground. About half of last Spring's work was done by the middle of April, just as new life was coming into the sprouts, and the remainder later in May, when the leaves were well developed. In the early grafting, not more than twenty or twenty-five per cent. of the scions grew, and these made a growth of from two to four feet; but of the later grafting, more than seventy-five per cent. have grown, although not making so strong a growth this season as the few of the earlier ones which survived. This certainly proves that, if the scions can be kept in good condition, late grafting is the proper thing for the Japan varieties in this latitude. I was not able to obtain any nuts of the very large, sweet Burbank, but of the two others I send a few samples.

The largest, light-colored one, marked "Early," while not so sweet as the Burbank, I consider of beautiful appearance, and fully as sweet as the average of our American varieties. When we consider that it will mature fully three weeks earlier than these, it must prove of very great value as a market sort. In a letter from Mr. Burbank, he speaks of it as being of medium size, excellent flavor, and so early that it is all gone before the American, Spanish or average Japan Chestnuts ripen. It is a fine, sweet nut, and has always produced a full crop, which ripens all at once.

I also send samples of the other, which is known as the eighteen-months' Chestnut, having been raised from seed of a Japan nut by Mr. Burbank, and come into fruiting in eighteen months after the seed was planted. It is certainly an early and profuse bearer, and, as you will see, a large nut of very fine appearance, and of better quality than any of the Europeans, or their crosses that I have found. It is a little later than the other, but still is earlier than most of our native Chestnuts here, and I came away from Meriden fully satisfied that Mr. Coe, in the purchase and development of these fine nuts, and his demonstration of the possibilities of utilizing our Chestnut sprout lands for commercial nut-growing in this way, was not only proving a public benefactor, but would also within a few years reap substantial profits from his great nut orchard, which is now so well under way.

Of one thing I am sure, that, in all this talk of commercial nut culture, we shall eventually settle down to the grafting and planting of the Japans and their seedlings, as they have a closer affinity for our American stocks than do any of the Europeans, while the quality of the best of them is fully equal to the sweetest of American nuts.

R. N. Y.—The nuts were very dry when they reached us, but the quality is excellent. The Early is fully as large as Paragon, and at least its equal in quality as judged by a single specimen.

NOTES FROM AMERICAN INSTITUTE FAIR.

NUTS, GRAPES AND VEGETABLES.

By Rural New Yorker.

One feature of the American Institute Fair that attracted much attention was the display of nuts made by *Parrys' Pomona Nurseries, Parry, N. J.* It comprised eighteen varieties of Chestnuts—**French, American Black, Persian, English Madeira and Japan Walnuts; Hickorynuts, Pecans, Filberts** and **Butternuts.** It showed the advance that has been made in nut-growing, and the interest manifested by visitors in the exhibit, showed that the public are anxious to learn about the subject. The size of several of the varieties of Chestnuts was a revelation to many. The quality of the nuts was left to the imagination, as "hands off" was the injunction. Yet some had sadly depleted the collection, the Superintendent saying that visitors would steal them in spite of everything.

Of the **Japan Chestnuts**, the following, given in the order of their ripening, are recommended by the firm: **Alpha**, said to be the earliest Chestnut known, is described as an upright, vigorous grower, coming into bearing at three years of age, and being very productive. Nuts large, four inches around, and two to three in a burr. It ripens September 5 to 10 without frost. **Beta** is an upright, vigorous grower, bearing at two to three years of age; very productive. Nuts large in size, two to three to the burr, ripening September 10 to 15, at the Pomona Nurseries. **Early Reliance** is of low, dwarf spreading habit, beginning to bear immediately, one-year grafts being frequently loaded. Nuts large, four inches in circumference, three to five nuts to the burr. The tree is said to be enormously productive, the nuts smooth, bright, uniform, attractive, ripening September 18 to 20. **Success** is given as larger than any of the others; tree an upright, vigorous grower; very productive. Nuts ripen September 20 to 23, but nothing is said as to their quality. **Parrys' Superb** is very highly praised, both in tree and fruit, and is recommended as a very valuable market sort. **Giant** is said to bear nuts measuring six inches in circumference, and running two to a burr. Tree a vigorous, upright grower, very productive; nuts smooth, dark and attractive. "The largest known Chestnut."

The **Spanish Chestnut** is described as a handsome, round-headed tree of rapid, spreading growth, that yields abundantly of large nuts of good quality, hence a desirable ornamental tree or profitable for market. **Ridgeley** is described as a large variety of the Spanish Chestnut from Delaware; very productive, and of good quality. **Numbo** and **Paragon** are both highly praised. The **Native Sweet** is placed at the end of the list, but is described as being unsurpassed for sweetness and quality.

The **Japan Walnut** is very highly recommended. It is claimed to be as hardy as the Oak, leaves of immense size and of a charming shade of green. The nuts are produced in abundance, in clusters of fifteen or twenty; they have shells thicker than those of the **Persian Walnut**, but not so thick as the **Black Walnut**. Meat sweet, of the best quality, flavor like a **Butternut**, but less oily and much superior. The trees are vigorous, of a handsome form, and need no pruning; they mature early, and bear young. The trees named are well worthy the attention of farmers. This country is paying for imported nuts something like $2,000,000 per year, the larger part of which should be kept at home.

The above Medals, also a Special Diploma, were awarded PARRYS' POMONA NURSERIES for the foregoing exhibit.

GRAFTED CHESTNUT TREES.

Without attempting to explain the reason why it is so, the fact is well known to every propagator of the improved varieties of the Chestnut that the grafted trees are very precocious, and will, as a rule, produce nuts when not more than two or three years old, while seedlings of the same rarely produce fruit under ten or twelve years. There is far more danger from over-fruitfulness than unproductiveness in grafted Chestnuts, for there are few persons who will have the courage to remove or thin out the crop of nuts on young trees, which is often necessary to prevent stunting the growth of the plants. It would be much better not to allow very young trees to bear at all, than to stunt their growth by over-bearing, but impatience to reap an early crop often ends in a half crop, or none.

I have on my farm two Chestnut trees, each about two feet in diameter, which were top grafted with **Paragon** scions, that produced the fourth year from grafts one hundred and twenty pounds of hulled nuts, one tree bearing fifty-nine pounds and the other sixty-one pounds, which sold at wholesale in Philadelphia at $10.00 per bushel.

Of the **Scott** Chestnut, Judge Scott, of Burlington, New Jersey, had one tree in a large field of wheat and realized from the crop of nuts, from the one tree, more than from the whole field of wheat.

The Albion Chestnut Company, Jno. J. Albertson, Secretary, Magnolia, Camden County, New Jersey, have a tract of one hundred and fifty acres of Chestnut sprout land, top grafted with the improved Japan and European varieties, divided into five-acre blocks, so as to have the benefit of intermixing the pollen of the various kinds and insure full crops. The varieties used of the European sorts are Cooper, Numbo, Paragon, Comfort, Shoemaker, Hannum, Scott, Corson and Ridgeley. Of the Japan sorts, Alpha, Beta, E. Prolific, Reliance and Parry's Giant, with a few assorted varieties for experiment.

From the small portion of the tract first grafted, they gathered the past season about forty bushels, principally of the Japans, which sold the first week in New York market at $14.00 per bushel; the next week at $10.00 per bushel. The following week the European varieties were sent, and sold for $8.00 per bushel. They are careful to keep each variety separate and distinct, with the object of supplying wood for grafting purposes.

Preparation for Market Chestnuts are best prepared for market by bathing in scalding water as soon as gathered and *thoroughly drying* till all surplus moisture is gone, so that moulding is avoided. The method is to place say a bushel of nuts in an ordinary washtub and on these pour boiling water in quantity sufficient to just cover the nuts an inch or two; the wormy nuts will float on the surface and are removed; in about ten to fifteen minutes the water will have cooled enough to allow the nuts to be removed by the hand; at this stage of the process the good of scalding has been accomplished, the eggs and larva of all insects have been destroyed, and the condition of the meat of the nut has been so changed that it will not become flinty hard in the curing for winter use. The water is drained off, nuts placed loosely in sacks, frequently turned and shaken up as they lay spread in sun or dry house, and after perfectly dry so as not to mould they may be packed in barrels or boxes and stored for winter, when they will be found very tender, sweet and delicious.

This process will also greatly hasten their ripening or coloring. They may be gathered by hand, and hulled while yet not colored and by scalding greatly improved in color and rushed into market one or two weeks in advance of their natural time, realizing much better prices.

Propagation. The general directions given under germination will apply to Chestnuts. They are stratified in sand, placed in a cool cellar and kept until Spring. The sand should be occasionally moistened to prevent its absorbing the moisture from the nuts. They may also be packed between layers of damp moss and placed in cellar until Spring, then planted in nursery rows, as previously described.

Budding and Grafting Chestnuts. BUDDING the Chestnut has not proven generally successful, though it is being done with partial success in California and some of the Southern States, the methods adopted being the shield and flute budding, and the best season of year is in August. The buds are freshly cut and immediately inserted with as little exposure as possible, wrapped carefully. In about three weeks the strings should be untied, loosened and retied, to prevent their cutting the tree. In the Spring following, the tops of the trees should be cut off above the bud and the bud allowed to make the growth; all suckers should be kept rubbed off. In New Jersey our success has not been such as to give much encouragement with this mode of propagation, though in sections where it will succeed it may be practiced, where the grafts set in the Spring have failed.

DORMANT BUDS, having been kept in cold storage, set in Spring as early as the bark would peel, have in some cases given satisfactory results.

GRAFTING, in its various styles, has given more universal satisfaction, though it is also attended with much uncertainty, its success being dependent upon so many conditions. The scions must have been cut in cold climates, before freezing weather, to insure them against injury from cold. In milder climates they may be allowed to remain on the trees until after cold weather and cut before the buds have moved, and kept in cool, moist place, neither too wet nor too dry. They should be kept in moss, free from sun and wind, during the operation of grafting, and waxed as fast as they are set, as a very little exposure at that time will prove fatal. After the above conditions have all been complied with, and everything seems favorable, we frequently have a few days of very warm weather before the scions have calloused and united with the stock, that will push out the buds, which will sometimes make a growth of four to six inches, and then wither and die for want of support. Both the cleft graft and whip graft are used, each according to the conditions. For top grafting in branches one inch or more in diameter the cleft graft is used; if the stock is two to three inches in diameter two grafts may be set to advantage; if both grow, they will the sooner heal over the wound, and after one season's growth the weaker one may be cut back. For small stocks less than one inch and for root grafting we prefer the whip or tongue graft. For very large stocks, with thick, heavy bark, the slip or bark graft is more successful. For description of each style, see under Grafting, page 42.

The best time to graft the Chestnut is in the Spring, just as the buds of the stock begin to swell, and may be continued, with dormant scions, until the leaves are half grown; before the buds have moved the scions may be cut from the tree and immediately set. For slip or bark grafting, however, it cannot be done so early, not until after the sap is running freely and the bark will peel readily and of course only with dormant scions.

From Rural New Yorker.

United States Pomologist Heiges says that the European Sweet Chestnut (*Castanea sativa*) has, for many years, been grafted in France and England upon the European black oak (*Quercus robur*), using young seedlings raised by planting the acorns where the trees are to remain permanently, or which have been freshly planted, and also upon branches of proper size on matured trees. Until quite recently, this has not been practiced in this country. The pomological division of the Department of Agriculture distributed scions of the Paragon, Numbo and Ridgely last Spring, and also in the Spring of last year. They were worked upon the Chestnut oak (*Quercus prinus*), and reports show as good success as when grafted on the native Chestnuts.

It is suggested that it may be possible to succeed with other species of oak as stocks, as, for example, the Post, Burr, Swamp, White oak, Yellow oak, Basket oak, all belonging to the same group as does the Chestnut oak. The success attained in Europe, Mr. Heiges says, by using the European Black oak as a stock, would indicate that our Black oak group might be equally available. This group comprises the Red, Scarlet, Pin, Spanish, Bear, Water, Shingle oak, etc., covering a vast area of country. Should several of these species be found to be suitable stocks for the Chestnut, the cultivation of this valuable nut would be much extended, as oaks will grow in soil and under conditions in which the roots of the native Chestnuts would die, if planted.

Our own experience does not correspond with the foregoing. We find nothing better than American Seedlings on which to graft the European and Japan varieties.

We have grafted them on Chestnut oaks and succeeded in getting them to take, and although they would make a fair growth the first year they would make an imperfect union and set an abundance of fruit buds indicating feeble constitution. The next year they put out a number of abortive burrs and died before the close of the year. Have not tried the other oaks named.

Insect Enemies

The Chestnut tree is seldom attacked by insects, though the weevil that infests the nuts is a very serious enemy, in some sections rendering the crop almost worthless.

A recent bulletin issued by the North Carolina Experiment Station, at Raleigh, gives the life history of the weevil, and suggests remedies for the pest. Its history is as follows:

The chestnut weevil is yellowish, with rusty spots and lines on the wing covers, and about the size of the common pea weevil. The footless grub is white or cream colored, with a red or yellowish head, about half an inch long when full grown; nearly cylindrical.

The winged beetles appear on the Chestnut trees about the time these begin to bloom, or a little after. The female lays her eggs by piercing the young ovary or husk, and deposits from one to four eggs in each. The eggs hatch in a few days. The shell of the nut subsequently forms and hardens around the grub. The holes seen in the shells of mature nuts are always made by an escaping grub, never by one entering. The number of eggs laid by each female is probably between fifty and one hundred. As soon as the eggs are laid, the winged insect dies, and no more are seen until the next Spring, there being but one brood a year. Under ordinary circumstances the grub escapes from the nut within ten days after the burr falls from the tree. It then enters the ground and changes to the pupa state, in which it remains dormant during the winter. In Spring it issues as a winged beetle. Here at the North the worms often remain alive in the nut during Winter, escaping in Spring.

No practical way has yet been found to circumvent the mischievous work of the beetle. All that at present can be suggested is to thoroughly handpick the nuts, sorting out those that show holes in the shell and feeding them to the hogs or turkeys. Wm. P. Corsa gives the following advice: To prevent the escape of the worms into the ground the nuts should be gathered as soon as they fall, and stored in tight boxes or bins from which the worms cannot escape. After twelve or fifteen days they may be killed by fumigating the box or bin with carbon bisulphide. Use eight ounces of this to a ton of nuts and cover the box or bin tightly for twenty-four hours. Then expose to the air until the carbon bisulphide has all evaporated. It will not hurt the edible nuts in the least. In short, Chestnut growers and Chestnut gatherers should make it an inviolable rule to kill every worm that they find in or out the nuts. And this is also a good rule for growers and gatherers of Pecans, Walnuts, Hazel and all other nuts to follow.

HOW TO DESTROY WORMS IN CHESTNUTS.

H. E. Van Deman, in Rural New Yorker.

The two species of Chestnut weevil known in North America infest the Chestnuts and Chinquapins in every locality where the latter grow naturally. Three methods of combating these enemies seem to me practical:

First, gather the nuts as they fall, and as soon as enough are on hand to warrant treatment, put them in a tight barrel, box or other receptacle that can be tightly covered. Procure a half pint or more of bisulphide of carbon, and pour some in an open cup, which should be placed with the nuts. It will permeate every space, and kill all the larvæ and eggs within thirty-six hours, if securely confined. It will not injure the nuts, either for eating or planting, if they are not longer subjected to treatment and are afterwards well aired. However, there is no danger from poisoning, except by inhaling the fumes. No fire should be allowed near, as the gas is very inflammable.

By the second method, as soon after gathering as possible put a large or small quantity of nuts into a basket or tub, and pour boiling water over them until all are covered an inch or more deep. Stir vigorously with a stick, and the light and faulty nuts will float, and may be skimmed off and fed to hogs to destroy the worms. Leave the good nuts in the water five minutes, when the eggs and little larvæ will be scalded. Pour off the water, or reheat it for another batch. Put the nuts in coarse sacks, only half filling them. Lay them in the best place to dry, shaking and turning often. The kernels of Chestnuts so treated will not be hard in Winter, but will not grow if planted.

Third, put in cold storage as soon as the nuts are gathered. This will prevent the development of the eggs, and for market dealers is feasible. The nuts may be taken out as the trade requires. A friend in the mountains of North Carolina told me that he had found by trial, that Chestnuts put in a box or sack, and buried in the earth a foot deep, did not become wormy, because the conditions (perhaps of temperature) were not agreeable to the hatching and growth of the insects.

In cases where wild trees or bushes of the Chestnut and Chinquapin abound, it is not possible to gather the wormy nuts as they fall, and destroy them, or to jar and catch, or otherwise materially to lessen the number of insects; but in isolated cases, these methods may be tried with hope of success.

7-13-95

The *Rural New Yorker* has given a description of the great Chestnut Orchard of H. M. Engle, at Marietta, Pa. Mr. Engle sends us this report of this year's prospect:

So far as tree growth in the forest is concerned, it is a success. Their bearing habit is also quite satisfactory, but the past few years the weevil has been unusually destructive. Should they continue thus, or get worse, Chestnut culture on sprout land would be discouraging. On planted trees, away from Chestnut timber land, we find very little damage from this cause.

It will be remembered that Mr. Engle's orchard is on "sprout land." The wild Chestnut trees were cut off, and improved varieties were grafted on the sprouts which grew from the stumps. It will be very unfortunate if an insect is able to offset, by its destructive work, the many advantages of this method.

Varieties

American.—Although we occasionally see in our markets very large and handsome specimens of the American Chestnut, there has been no, or but little, effort to improve this worthy species.

Hathaway.—Originated with Mr. B. Hathaway, of Michigan, and is described as a very large and handsome variety; a strong, vigorous grower, and productive.

Phillips.—A large and handsome variety, of excellent flavor, with a very smooth, dark-brown shell. Originated with Whitman Phillips, at Ridgewood, New Jersey.

Pennell.—From Joseph Pennell, of Delaware County, Pennsylvania; a large, handsome tree; very productive; nut medium size; good quality and very early.

Mather.—From Montgomery County, Pennsylvania; a very large tree; very productive; nuts good size, smooth, dark and handsome, with very little fuzz, but its great merit is in its extreme earliness, maturing its crop early in September and long in advance of any other Americans.

EUROPEAN CHESTNUTS.

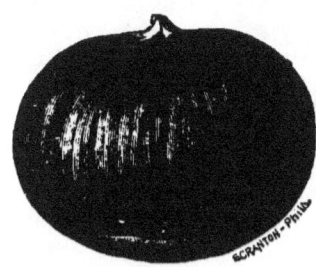

SPANISH.

The **European Chestnut** has been grown in this country a half century or more, with indifferent success, very few of the original importations surviving the extreme cold weather of our Middle and Northern States. From these few, or from their seedlings, have been selected some very valuable varieties. They have found a congenial home in Eastern Pennsylvania and Delaware, and are largely grown for market. They make a handsome low-headed tree. The nuts are larger than the American; bright, brown color; coarser flesh, not so sweet nor so good quality as the American, with less fuzz and more or less astringency or bitterness of skin. I will name some of the most desirable of the European strain, of American origin, or American seedlings of European varieties.

Comfort.—Origin: Pennsylvania, near Germantown, and from its close resemblance in tree, foliage, habit of growth, burrs, nuts and other characteristics to the **Paragon**, with its history and circumstances in connection with it, we are led to believe the Comfort was the mother of the famous Paragon. Burrs very large, broad, flattened; nuts broad; shell covered with thin hairy fuzz; quality good. Tree very productive; generally three to the burr.

Cooper.—Tree a vigorous-grower and very productive; burr large; nut large, smooth and glossy, with little fuzz; quality very good; grown largely in vicinity of New Jersey and in Camden county, N. J.

Corson.—From Walter H. Corson, Plymouth Meeting, Montgomery county, Pennsylvania. Burrs of large size, nuts very large; usually three in a burr; shell dark brown, somewhat ridged; some fuzz about the point. A very valuable variety, of good quality and very productive.

Dager.—Originated near Wyoming, Delaware, from seed of Ridgely. Claimed to be larger and better than its parent.

Dupont (Miller's).—From seedlings of the many trees imported by the Duponts of Wilmington, (of powder fame), there have been selected a number of valuable varieties, of which Miller's is one. Tree very productive; nut medium size and of fair quality.

Eureka.—From Kentucky. Quality above the average of European type.

Hannum.—(Styer) (Concord). Originated at Concordville, Penna. Tree very strong; upright grower and attains immense size; enormously productive. One to three nuts in a burr; nuts of good size, bright color and very good quality.

Marron.—This name is applied to a class of Chestnuts imported from France, one of the best of which is Marron *Combale*, resembling the Japan type.

Moncar.—A seedling of Ridgely. Originated near Dover, Delaware. Described as smaller and better quality than its parent.

Numbo.—Originated with Mahlon Moon, Morrisville, Penna., from seed of an imported tree. Tree a good grower; close, compact head; burrs medium sized and pointed; nuts large, smooth and pointed, with fuzz around the stem; quality good; valuable.

Ridgeley.—This is also a seedling from Mr. Dupont's importation. Tree is of immense size and very productive, more than five bushels of nuts, selling at $11.00 per bushel, having been gathered from the original tree in a single season; burrs of medium size, and carry from two to three nuts each; nut of medium size, with some fuzz at point; kernel sweet and of good quality.

Paragon.—Originated from a seed planted by Mr. Shaeffer, of Germantown, Philadelphia, Pennsylvania, and introduced by H. M. Engle, Marietta, Pennsylvania, and probably has done more to stimulate the interest in Chestnut culture than any other one variety, and to Mr. Engle is due great credit for placing it before the public. From the fact that it originated near the home of the Comfort and so strikingly resembles it, we are led to believe the Paragon is a seedling of the Comfort. Burrs of immense size, distinctly flattened on top; nuts large, three to five in a burr, and covered with fine hairy fuzz; kernel fine-grained, sweet and of good quality.

PARAGON.

Scott.—Grown by Judge Scott, of Burlington, whose father many years ago bought from a nursery three Spanish Chestnut trees, planted them in a row about thirty feet apart, and the one from which this nut is grown happened to be in the middle. It is now a large tree, the trunk about five feet in diameter. It is a regular and heavy bearer. The Judge has propagated and planted an orchard of this variety, and claims among its important features large size and early bearing; two-year grafts generally produce nuts; immense productiveness and good quality; beautiful, glossy mahogany  color, freedom from fuzz and an almost entire exemption from the attacks of the Chestnut weevil. While the crop of two trees standing on either side of the Scott is badly damaged by worms, it is the exception to find a wormy nut among the Scott.

JAPANESE CHESTNUTS.

The Japan Chestnut makes a smaller tree than either the American or European, with slender branches and long narrow leaves.

They appear to thrive over a wide range of the United States, probably not so far north as the other species, but possibly may extend the culture of Chestnuts farther south, even into Central Florida.

The seedlings assume such a wide range in character, from very large to very small, very early to medium season, that we may hope to develop some very valuable varieties from this great acquisition. Among those already put on the market are the following:

Among their valuable features are their early bearing, early ripening, great productiveness, large size, smooth shells free from fuzz.

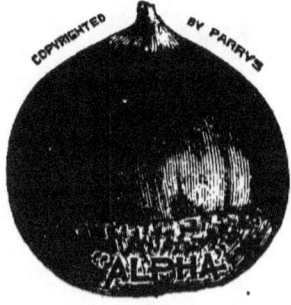

Alpha.—The earliest known Chestnut. Originated with *Parrys' Pomona Nurseries*, from seed of Parry's Giant. Tree an upright, vigorous grower; very productive; the original tree began to bear at three years, and has never failed to produce a good crop. Nuts large, running two to three to the burr; opening from 5th to 10th of September, without the aid of frost, and commanding highest prices in market.

Beta.—From *Parrys' Pomona Nurseries*, from seed of Parrys' Giant. Very similar to above, ripening immediately after it.

Biddle—From *J. W. Kerr*, Denton, Md. Large burr, containing three to five nuts; nuts large, light brown.

Black.—From *J. W. Kerr*, Denton, Md. Very large, productive and early.

Col. Martin.—From *J. W. Kerr*, Denton, Md. Nuts large; burrs large, three to five to the burr.

Early Prolific.—From *J. T. Lovett*, Little Silver, N. J. Ripening soon after Beta. Medium size and very prolific.

Felton.—From *J. W. Killen*, Felton, Del. Nut large and sweet.

Kerr.—From *J. W. Kerr*, Denton, Md. Large, dark-colored nut, usually two and three in a burr. Burr has very few and short spines; very productive.

PARRYS' SUPERB.

Parrys' Superb.—Seedling of Parrys' Giant from *Parrys' Pomona Nurseries*, Parry, N. J. Immensely productive, making a mass of burrs each, generally containing three very large, complete, handsome nuts; ripening mid-season.

Killen.—From *J. W. Killen*, Felton, Delaware, A remarkably large and handsome nut of very good quality. Three to the burr.

Parson's Japan.—Nuts large, one and one-half inches broad; dark, glossy brown; quality good.

Parrys' Giant.—From *Parrys' Pomona Nurseries*, Parry, N. J. The largest known variety. Two to two and a half inches across. Seldom more than one to the burr. Smooth, dark color and handsome; ripening mid-season.

PARRYS' GIANT.

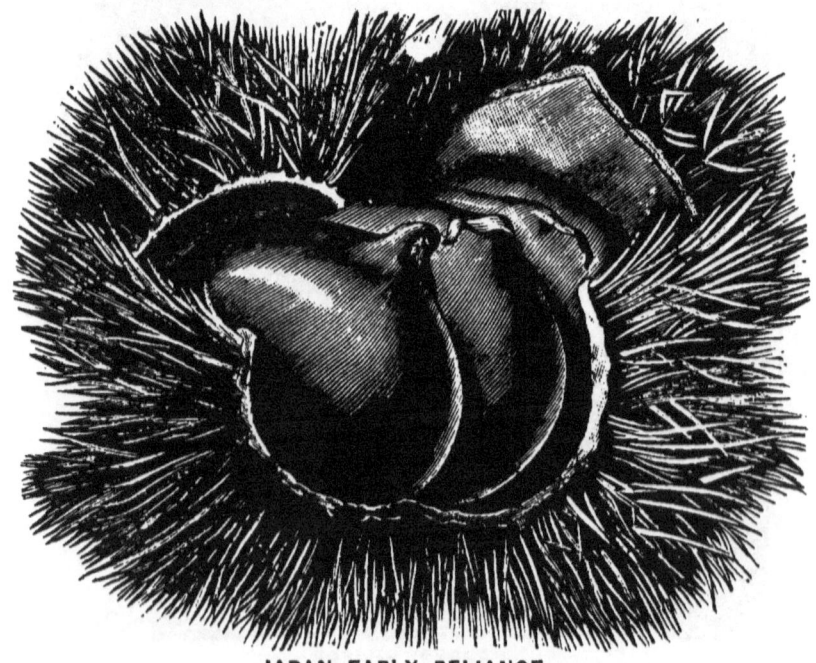

JAPAN EARLY RELIANCE.

Reliance.—Seedling of Parrys' Giant, from *Parrys' Pomona Nurseries*, Parry, N. J. Tree of dwarf, spreading habit, very productive and so very precocious that it frequently produces nuts the same season the grafts are set. Nuts large, uniform and ripen early.

Success.—Seedling of Parrys' Giant, from *Parrys' Pomona Nurseries*, Parry, N. J. Large, handsome nuts, ripening mid-season.

CHINQUAPIN.

Although we occasionally meet with some very fine specimens of Chinquapin in the market, there has been but little effort made to improve this species.

To the late A. S. Fuller we are indebted for scions, which were grafted on to the native Chestnut, and are making good growth, of a superior Chinquapin, with the following description, which bears his honored name.

CHINQUAPIN.

Fuller—Leaves large, broadly oval, pointed, coarsely serrate, pale green above, clear silvery white below. Burrs in long racemes, very large for this species; spines long, strong, branching and sharp. Nuts, only one in each burr, rather short, broad, top-shaped, with blunt point; shell very smooth, glossy and almost black; kernel fine grained and sweet. Ripens early.

Emerson.—From *P. Emerson*, Wyoming, Delaware. A very large, handsome nut of fine quality.

Rush.—From *John G. Rush*, of West Willow, Pennsylvania. A very large nut, the size of the American Chestnut, with which it is supposed to be a hybrid; very fine quality, with true Chinquapin flavor.

HAZELNUTS OR FILBERTS.—(*Corylus.*)

Of Hazelnuts there are several species, most of which are low shrubs or bushes, though one attains the size of forest trees. They are unisexual, having the staminate blossoms in catkins, and appear in early Fall of the previous year's growth, and in March or April following the pollen is distributed. The pistillate blossom, which is a star-like tuft, is sometimes not developed in time to become fertilized, and a failure of the crop is the result.

The cultivation of the Hazelnut in this country has not been very encouraging, principally on account of the plants being attacked by a fungus or blight which destroys the plant.

Propagation The Hazel may be propagated by seed, layers, suckers, cuttings, or by grafting. They grow very readily from cuttings or layers, which is probably the best means of propagation.

For fruiting orchard, a light loam, with dry subsoil, will give best results. Strong, rich or wet land produces an excessive growth of wood with but little fruit, and also renders them more liable to blight.

In England, where the Hazel is a very important crop, the nuts are gathered just before fully ripe, and marketed in the husks. They are generally used for table purposes only, though an oil resembling olive oil is sometimes expressed from it. In other parts of Europe it is used in various ways, some making bread from it as from Chestnuts.

The **American Hazel** grows naturally through the Middle and New England States, in the Mississippi Valley, and on the Pacific Slope.

The **Hazels** are very free from insect enemies, though a nut weevil is reported on the American species.

Varieties Of the long list of Hazelnuts introduced in this country I give some of the most promising.

Bond Nut.—Husk hairy and short; nut of medium size, oblong; shell thin; kernel large; very productive.

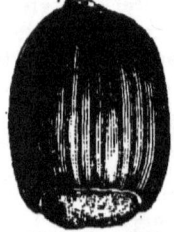

KENTISH COB.

Cosford Thin-Shelled.—Husk hairy; nut large, oblong; shell of light brown color, very thin; kernel large and excellent; ripens early and is very productive.

Kentish Cob (*Lambert*).—Husk nearly smooth; nut large, oblong and slightly compressed; shell rather thick, of brown color; kernel full and rich. A very valuable nut.

HICKORIES.—(*Hicoria.*)

The Hickory is a noble tree of large size and handsome form, with compound serrate leaves, with an odd number of leaflets varying in number and arranged on opposite sides of the leaf stalk. They produce their male and female flowers together, developed from one bud. The male flowers are slender, pendulous, in clusters of three, issuing from the base of the terminal bud of the previous season's growth. Female flowers form on the end of the new growth, from which the nuts are produced.

PECAN.—(*Hicoria Pecan—Carya Oliveformis.*)

The **Pecan** is by far the most valuable of the Hickory family and is indigenous to the Mississippi Valley as far North as Iowa, and Southern Central United States; rarely found along the Atlantic Coast, but luxuriating in a congenial climate along the alluvial river bottoms of Texas and Louisiana, though it will adapt itself to almost any locality if given good rich soil, on which it makes rapid growth and attains great size, four to six feet in diameter, with fifty to seventy-five feet spread of branches, and seventy-five to one hundred feet in height, towering above the surrounding tree tops.

The largest nuts, with thinnest shells, are found in Mississippi, Louisiana and Texas, where they grow in abundance in strips of woodland bordering the streams and moist lands. It does not object to an occasional overflow if not too long inundated.

Wherever the Hickory will grow it will be safe to plant the Pecan, though the best nuts are produced in the long summers of the warmer climates. The *Rural New Yorker* says: "No State has the monopoly of Pecan Culture. It will pay in forty-three other States as well as Texas."

Orchard Planting There has been a great diversity of opinion in regard to the best mode of starting a Pecan grove. Some still claim that the proper plan is to plant the nut where the tree is to grow and remain, so as not to disturb the tap root, while most of those of large experience now assert it is best to plant the seed in the seed bed, then transfer to nursery row, as previously described, and at one year root prune, which will produce the lateral rootlets and after transplanted will the more quickly come to bearing.

Probably the largest planted orchard of Pecans is that of *F. A. Swinden*, Brownwood, Texas, who has eleven thousand trees planted on four hundred acres. These were large selected soft shell nuts, planted forty feet apart each way, where the tree was to remain. Of this four hundred acres, one hundred acres are eight years old; one hundred acres six to seven years old; one hundred acres four to five years old, and one hundred acres two to three years old. The first planting is beginning to produce nuts. Mr. Swinden has grown cotton, corn and vegetables among the trees. And not only have these cultivated crops been a source of profit, but the trees in the meantime have made good growth.

Louis Brediger, Idlewild, Texas, has five hundred trees grown from nuts, planted where the trees are to stand.

W. R. Stuart Estate, Ocean Springs, Miss., has one hundred bearing trees in cultivation, and five hundred trees coming to bearing, a large portion of which are choice grafted varieties.

H. S. Kedney, of Winter Park, Fla., has an orchard of four thousand trees, covering one hundred acres, at Monticello, Fla., of grafted varieties. Throughout Florida there are a number of Pecan groves, though mostly of seedlings.

In California you occasionally meet groves of five hundred to six hundred trees, while on the Atlantic Coast there have been but few plantings. At Federalsburg, Md., there is a grove of one hundred and fifty trees, seven years planted, which is making vigorous growth. In Virginia there are some individual trees producing good crops. Further up the coast, at Milford, Del., is a fine large tree that seldom fails. At the Lorillard Stock Farm, Burlington county, N. J., are two very large trees producing annually heavy crops of good sized nuts, and there are a number of young trees growing in the county that have not yet come to bearing. They are reported as growing finely in Northern New York and New England States, though they have not come to fruiting. And it may be that the tree will grow in northern latitude and withstand the low temperature and produce no fruit, on account of the male and female flowers not developing at the same time.

As the Pecan is grown only on this continent, and we have the whole world for our market, it is difficult to estimate the importance or value of this production, when we consider the area of country adapted to its culture, the ease with which it is produced, and the susceptibility of improvement by selection, in size of nut, cracking quality, thinness of shell and flavor of meat.

Propagation. As the Pecans, like other nuts and fruits, cannot be depended on to reproduce the exact types from seed, the only safe plan to secure any desired variety is by budding, grafting, layers, cuttings or suckers. Should it be impossible or impracticable to procure plants thus propagated, and the planter is content with seedling trees, which may also prove profitable, there should be great care exercised in selecting the nuts, which until recently has been the only style of trees planted. With this method the important features to be considered are large size, thin shells, plump kernel and easily extracted, good quality, and from vigorous trees of productive habit.

The Pecan may be propagated very readily from root cuttings, or by severing the roots of growing trees the detached roots will send up suckers, which, of course, will be the same as the original tree.

Budding and Grafting
The Pecan may be budded or grafted upon any of the Hickories. The modes having proven the most successful in the Southern States are the annular or ring-budding, root-grafting and cleft-grafting at the collar, as previously described for the various processes. The grafting should be done early in the Spring, just as the buds begin to swell. For annular budding the operation should be deferred until July or August.

PROPAGATING HICKORIES.

A New Jersey subscriber wrote to the editor of *Garden and Forest* as follows: "How shall I go to work to propagate in quantity different varieties of the Hickory—for example, some which bear remarkably large and thin-shelled nuts? I have been told that it is next to impossible to graft them." The editor made the following reply:

We have referred this inquiry to Mr. Jackson Dawson, who says that although he has never tried to graft a Hickory out of doors, and it is true that these trees are somewhat difficult subjects, nevertheless he does not hesitate to say that with proper stock and precaution they can be as readily propagated under glass as most of the so-called difficult plants. He has experimented with most of the species and has succeeded with all he has tried. This success with several species and varieties of Hickory has been gained without any special preparation of the stock, and, in fact, most of the time he has gone to the woods and dug up the stock after he had received the scions. Of course, this made the work still more uncertain, and yet in the worst cases he has saved twenty-five or thirty per cent. of the grafts.

"My method," writes Mr. Dawson, "has been to side-graft, using a scion with part of the second year's wood attached, binding it firmly and covering it with damp sphagnum until the union has been made. The best time I have found for the operation, under glass, has been during February, and the plants have been kept under glass until midsummer and wintered the first year in a cold frame. In all genera I find certain species which may be called free stocks—that is, stocks which take grafts more readily than others. Thus, nearly all the oaks will graft readily on *Quercus Rober;* the birches will graft more easily on *Betula alba* than on others; so of the Hickories, observation has led me to believe that the best stock is the bitter nut, *hicoria minima*. This species grows twice as rapidly as the common Shag-bark Hickory, and while young the cambium is quite soft. I should advise any one who wishes to propagate Hickories on a large scale to grow stock of this species in boxes not more than four inches deep. In this way all the roots can be saved and there will be no extreme tap root, and when shaken out of the boxes the plants are easily established in pots and ready for grafting. If taken up in the ordinary way from the woods it requires almost two years to get them well rooted, and often the stocks die for want of roots after the graft has really taken. If grown in rich soil the stocks will be large enough to use in one or two years. I should then pot them early in the Fall, keeping them from heavy frosts and bringing them into the house about the first of January, and as soon as they begin to make roots I should side-graft them close to the collar and plunge them in sphagnum moss, leaving the top bud of the graft out to the air. The graft ought to be well united about the last of March, when the plants should be taken from the sphagnum and set in the body of the house to finish their growth. After carrying them over the next Winter in a cold pit they could be planted out the following Spring, and the second year they could be set where they are to remain, unless they are transplanted every second year."

PECAN CULTURE.

W. R. Stuart, in American Farm News.

Our friend, Dr. H. L. Stewart, of Tecumseh, Mich., has handed me your valuable paper, July, 1892, requesting me to send you what I can conveniently on "Pecan Culture."

Fifteen years ago (at the age of fifty-six years) I was impressed with the belief that Pecan culture in the Southern half of the United States promised vast possibilities if due care and attention were given it. I purchased and planted the largest and best flavored Pecans that could be found, without regard to price. Experience has demonstrated the correctness of that theory. And it was in this way that a new industry—Pecan culture—was begun; an industry new not only to myself, but new to the country at large. During the years which have followed, I have felt a deep interest in this work, and have used every honorable means at my command to advance the cause by improving the varieties grown and by bringing the subject prominently before the American people.

Some writers have been pleased to call me the "Father of Pecan Culture." If my humble efforts have been instrumental in giving this branch of horticulture the prominence it has attained, surely those years were well spent, and I have reason to be proud of the distinction accorded me. For the Pecan has taken its place in the front rank as the best and most profitable of nut-bearing trees, while the nut itself, where its merits are fully known, is pronounced superior to all others. And this industry must go on from year to year increasing in popular favor, as well as in profit to those engaged in its pursuit. The pride felt in this work has been seasoned with a reasonable admixture of profit and pleasure; but there is an even greater pleasure in the thought that I may have rendered valuable service to those of my fellow beings whom I have induced to engage in Pecan culture.

The Pecan belongs to the family of Hickory, and is found growing in its wild state, (very varied as to quality and productiveness), from the gulf to the lakes, and principally in the rich soil along the Wabash, Missouri, Mississippi and many rivers in Texas and Arkansas, where it attains in fact its largest growth, often measuring three to four feet in diameter, with a spread of top sixty to seventy feet. Many years ago some nuts were planted in Maryland, and now some of the finest trees in the Union may be found growing there. Its habit is lower and more spreading than the Hickory, when not too much surrounded by other trees; growing out alone it makes a full oval head, forming one of the handsomest of shade trees, with foliage a rich dark green in color, and under favoring conditions of very rapid growth. The nuts are borne in clusters of three to as many as seven on the extremities of the new wood; the staminate flowers appearing at the ends of the preceding year's growth.

The best time, perhaps, for planting trees is in the Fall, from November 1 to the middle of December, or as soon as they have shed their leaves in the Fall; Spring planting from February 1 until the buds begin to swell in the Spring. The nuts may be planted any time to advantage from season of ripening until late in the Spring, varied by condition in latitude; the middle of March the latest admissible period usually; the greater delay in time of planting, always remember, the greater necessity for thorough previous soaking of the nuts in water, from two to six days before putting into the ground; plant in rows about ten inches apart, covering three inches deep; put fertilizers three inches under the nuts; cultivate well by keeping the ground level and clean. If not desirable to plant out permanently at one year, root prune them in the row by running a sharp spade under and cutting the tap root eighteen inches below the surface as soon in the Fall after the leaves have fallen as practicable; this will tend to develop a strong growth of lateral or branch roots, and when finally removed to their permanent place, either in two or three years, it can be done with little if any loss. If the nuts are planted where the tree is to stand permanently, the soil should be loosened to the depth of two feet for a space of three feet in diameter and well fertilized, especially around the outside. Plant three or four nuts in a place, covering about three inches deep and thinning out in the Fall, leaving the strongest. Pecans have an off year; therefore, when planting a grove of five hundred trees, plant one hundred trees every year for five years; you will then have fruit every year.

The most advantageous soil is best indicated by observing the conditions where the Pecan or Hickory naturally thrive. Its habit is usually on made alluvial lands or river bottoms, where the soil is rich, deep, friable, moist, but not water-soaked, except from an occasional overflow, an event by no means unfavorable to its thrift when not too prolonged or of over-frequent occurrence; still as a tree it adapts itself and will succeed satisfactorily in growth and bearing in a varying degree upon every class of soils, and the writer has seen good results both on thin, sandy lands and upon the pine flats; unquestionably, however, the deep alluviums or river lands, even those liable to occasional overflow, and such as are in consequence of little value for other purposes, constitute those of the greatest value to plant the Pecan upon, and we draw special attention to a fact of such deep significance. For the rest it is not advisable to select land to plant on with too compact a subsoil, likely to hold surface water or keeping the roots soaked beneath too continuously, though even these least desirable of all lands to plant on are not barren of good results. A happy mean in respect to moisture afforded is the point to aim at, and a fertility, natural if it be possible, or otherwise approximated by due and regular addition of fertilizers. It is self-evident that the Pecan calls for an equal draft upon the soil as would a crop of corn. The Pecan is a gross feeder; you cannot expect to raise a premium crop of the latter without a fertile soil, and in this respect the Pecan is exactly similar in its requirements.

The cultivation should be thorough. It is best to grow some crop the first four or five years. Cotton, if you are located in the cotton growing belt, or any crop that requires clean culture will do, and by mulching around the tree when the trees are come into bearing the orchard may be turned into a pasture. But the treatment of a Pecan orchard should not differ much from that of an apple orchard or an orange grove. I know trees here that are thirteen years old, bearing from one barrel to one barrel and a half of nuts, and are one foot in diameter, and others of same age not four inches in diameter. So much for care and cultivation.

Trees should not be planted less than forty feet apart, sixty and seventy feet, according to the natural fertility of the soil, to insure the most lasting results in form and fruit for the succeeding years.

The Pecan begins to bear a few nuts at six to seven years of age, but at ten years if the trees have had good care and soil to grow in you may expect a paying crop, increasing annually until the tree arrives at a mature bearing age, in thirty to forty years.

PECAN AND FRUIT CULTURE.

Herbert Post, in the Southern Florist and Gardener.

The people who have never made a study of nut and fruit culture have no idea what these industries are worth to the country.

When lands that are unsalable at $5 per acre can be made in ten years or less to be worth $1,000 per acre, with continued increase for years, it is worth investigation.

What we state here are facts, with abundant proof.

Twenty years ago the land on which the city of Riverside, Cal., now stands, was a pasture, the land not worth five dollars per acre—now worth thousands. Only twelve years ago the total shipment of fruits and nuts from California did not exceed five hundred car loads. In 1893 they reached the enormous amount of twenty-five thousand car loads, and are increasing every year.

Last year, at Willows, Cal., a man sold his crop of Cherries, grown on four and one-half acres, for $2,300, the money being paid before the purchaser gathered the crop. Here is $541 per acre earnings, with little or no expense.

It is not uncommon for lands in nuts and fruits in California to earn from $300 to $600 per acre.

Southern Oregon reports sales of Apples from ten acres last season for $4,650.

About ten years ago W. W. Stringfellow, of Hitchcock, Texas, started fifteen acres in Pears, and on land not worth $20 per acre.

Last year he stated to a reporter that he had four thousand four hundred Pear trees, one thousand of which were in bearing. He said, judging from past crops, he would have fifteen bushels to the tree, or fifteen thousand bushels for sale. For these fifteen acres of four thousand four hundred trees, he had been offered and refused $75,000, or $5,000 per acre.

We believe that the Southern States have capabilities in fruit, vegetable and nut culture now little dreamed of. Being one thousand five hundred miles nearer the market than California, there is a large profit in the saving of transportation alone for the South. No fear of overstocking the market when some of the cities take and dispose of forty to sixty car loads daily, consumption keeping pace with production. California and Florida products are now being shipped to Europe with success. In many of the smaller villages of the United States these fruits are found on sale, as well as in the larger cities. But in nothing has there been greater interest manifested of late years than the Pecan industry, which shows greater profit than any fruit. This industry has all the elements of profit at very little cost, risk or insects, which are a great drawback to fruit growing. Most ripe fruits must be hurried into market as rapidly as possible, to prevent loss by decay. With the Pecan, they can be kept twelve months perfectly sweet, the grower choosing his market at his leisure. A favorite nut everywhere, all, or nearly all, of which are grown and consumed in the United States, but very few finding their way abroad. There is a security in growing Pecans, which, at their small cost of planting, makes a grove unequalled by any investment in stocks or bonds, and the beauty about it is that any one having but a few acres of land can plant a fortune, which is as sure as the promise that "seed time and harvest shall never fail."

The owner of a good Pecan grove can count on large earnings after the trees are ten years old, continuing to increase for thirty years, and last the lifetime of many generations.

The young trees begin to bear at the age of six years, and pay well at eight, when they are planted in groves, which is the best way to grow them. Thousands of acres of unused land in the South, on which the owner pays taxes and receives no income, can be made the most valuable acres on the farm by planting them in Pecans.

The time is near at hand when nut and fruit growing will be conducted on a much larger scale than now, and on business principles, for it has been found that for clean profit no branch of farm products pays so well. At Acampo, Cal., is a ranch of one thousand and fifteen acres, which contains the following varieties of nuts and fruits: Thirty-four thousand Almond trees, ten thousand Peach trees, eight thousand Olive trees, seven thousand Prunes, three thousand Apricots, three thousand Figs, one thousand Pears, nine hundred Orange, five hundred Cherry, five hundred Plum and sixteen thousand table and raisin Grape vines.

The revenue from this place is enormous, and it is conducted with as much care in detail as a large mercantile house. The advantages of conducting such enterprises on a large scale are superior. Buyers will come to the farm and buy and gather the crops themselves, or if sold on the market by the owner he can select his markets. This is in no sense "fancy farming." It is common sense with business principles. So far as we know, no nut or fruit grower has been compelled to mortgage his crop for advances, like the grower of cotton. The advantages possessed by Pecan culture over that of fruit are very great. To bring an Orange grove up to bearing costs about $200 per acre. In strong contrast we have the Pecan, which can be planted for $3 per acre, for the best thin-shell nuts, and the ground between the trees can be made to earn a good deal of money by growing small fruits.

The Pecan can be grown with profit in every State in the Union, on any good soil capable of growing any trees, as the deep growing tap root feeds upon soil untouched by other trees.

In the matter of purchasing Pecan trees where the tap root was cut, a great mistake has been made. The cutting of the root has destroyed its bearing qualities. It will make a good shade tree, but as a nut bearer it will disappoint its owners.

When there exists a sub-soil, as in most soils, it pays to loosen up the earth with dynamite, which is but small expense, but gives the young trees rapid growth. Planting the Pecan in ordinary soils, it requires two or three years' growth for the roots to force their way through the compact sub-soil. When the young tree is twelve inches above ground the roots are three to four feet below.

A TREATISE ON NUT CULTURE.

By using dynamite for loosening the soil, the tree will in the same length of time have grown from four to five feet above, with roots proportionately deep.

The cost per tree for the dynamite should not exceed twenty cents, and it has accomplished a work which benefits the tree for years.

No American tree has so few insect enemies as the Pecan. Here we have none worthy of notice. The sap and leaf have an acrid taste, which repels such insects as infest most trees.

A great advantage in planting the Pecan nuts is that you can see what you plant, and can depend upon the product of your trees being same as seed planted. Professor Steele says fully ninety per cent. (if not one hundred) can be depended upon. This is better as well as cheaper than to buy the trees, even if all right.

Cultivated trees bear with more regularity than those of wild growth. We have the wild trees, that we know have borne annual crops for the past six years in succession. The Pecan will grow to the height of seventy-five feet, with wide spreading branches, is symmetrical in shape, with very luxuriant dark-green foliage, late in coming out in the Spring, but retaining its leaves until late in the Fall.

While of the same family as the Black Walnut and Hickory, the Pecan is of a lower spreading habit than the latter, making a denser shade. The wood is just as valuable for use as the hickory, and very much like it in its texture.

Planting thirty-five by thirty-five feet apart is a good distance for permanent growth, but very much can be added in profit per acre for ten or twelve years by planting another Pecan tree in center of each square, which will give you sixty-one trees per acre. Until the trees are large enough for the limbs to touch each tree adjoining, you are receiving the earnings of twenty-five trees in addition. When necessary, the center trees can be cut out, and you have then thirty-six trees left per acre, which, by this time, should yield as great earnings as the whole sixty-one will in the earlier years of growth.

From the growing interest in Pecan culture in all sections of the country, it is evident that the people appreciate the value of these trees as money producers. The small cost of starting a grove, their long life, surety of bearing, requiring but little care or expense, being so largely in their favor over other nut or fruit trees. A grove of only ten acres, planted in the best thin shell, will earn more than fifty acres in ordinary crops.

FORT WORTH, TEXAS.

PECAN GROWING IN LOUISIANA.

BOLTING A BIG NUT STORY.

How The Laugh Was Turned on the Croakers.

By Samuel H. James, in Rural New Yorker.

In my rambles around New Orleans, when a student at Tulane University, in that city, I took close notice of the various products offered for sale, and the prices charged for them. I soon saw that the most valuable of all the horticultural and agricultural products—the one that brought the most money for the given weight—was the large sized soft-shell Louisiana pecans. The best grade of these sold at the unvarying price of $1 a pound, and as years went on there was no decline in the price. I had spent much of my boyhood upon a cotton plantation, where pecans thrived, and I knew that a tree came into bearing at nine years old, and would bear a profitable crop at fifteen years. One day I did a little sensible reasoning on this subject. I was still a young man. If I bought a large number of these nuts and planted a big grove, ten years afterwards I would still be in the middle life, and have a valuable source of profit. Every old man whom I had ever heard talk on this subject had expressed a regret that he had not planted a Pecan grove in his youth. I determined that this should not be my regret in old age. I resolved to save enough of my yearly allowance to buy me a large amount of seed of these extra-size Pecans. My mother owned a plantation in Louisiana, and after some persuasion she agreed to give me enough land to plant my Pecan grove on. As this was rich alluvial land, there was nothing now in my way to prevent my beginning my work. I planted my grove nine years ago this winter, and last fall it came into bearing. It was a happy day for me when I first saw the clusters of nuts hanging on the trees. My grove now numbers about seventy acres, and this winter I shall plant thirty acres more.

How Old Timers Laughed.

When I first started to plant my grove nine years ago, I became the laughing stock of the whole community. I was doing something no one had ever done before, and it was past comprehension to our people how any one could wait ten years to get paid for his work. Fun was poked at me at every turn and corner, even by my best friends. I planted the nuts in the open field among the cotton, and my friends would say, "Why! there is no possible hope of your getting a Pecan grove. The little negroes will grabble up the nuts before they come up, and even if they do germinate, the mules and plows and careless negroes will destroy them all before they are a year old." One old uncle, who thought he was very wise in such matters, said that if I did such foolish things as this I would be sold out at sheriff's sale before the Pecans came into bearing. None of these things ever happened, and although the last years have been very disastrous to cotton planters, our financial condition is better to-day than when I planted the Pecan grove, and would be better still had I done more of it.

How the Grove Was Planted.

And now the laugh, which nine years ago was very loud and strong, has been turned, and, instead of a foolish thing, my friends see that it was a wise thing I did. There was one neighbor, a good farmer withal, but a man with the bad trait of thinking that all men who did differently from him were in the wrong. This man lost no opportunity of poking fun at me nine years ago, when I was planting my grove. Nine years have passed since then, and that makes a great difference. I was passing by his house the other day, and I saw that he had torn down his yard fence in order to cut down a fine oak tree that was shading a Pecan tree his wife had planted years ago. I stopped to have a talk with him. "I am one of the biggest fools that ever lived," he said. "When my wife planted this one tree, I should have planted half my place in Pecans."

I planted the nuts in the cotton rows thirty feet apart, and the rows sixty feet apart. I marked each nut with three pieces of shingle. When the trees were one year old I put a stout post by each tree, which was removed in six years, as the trees were then large enough to take care of themselves. For the first five years I planted the ground to cotton, then alternated it with corn and peas. My trees now average about twenty-five feet high, and in a few more years I shall have to sow the land with clover, and use it for pasture. The trees on our rich land should stand sixty by sixty feet, so I will have to remove some of mine, as they are too thick in the row. But I shall wait and see which bear the finest nuts, and remove only the inferior ones. This will give a little unevenness, but will cause me to save all the finer nut-bearers, which could not be done if every other tree were removed.

I have several trees in the yard at Cottage Oaks, just six years in advance of my big grove, and from these I can make a fair comparison of what my grove will do in six years. In the Fall of 1892 several of these trees bore as much as a barrel apiece, so in five more years I can count on many of my trees in the grove doing as much. From my experience with Pecans, I have found out the following facts: Trees grown from fine nuts reproduce themselves, with slight variations. The cutting of the tap root of a Pecan tree does not prevent its bearing. It causes the tree to grow more slowly, and to produce a denser head, with more fruit-bearing twigs, which will bear twice as many nuts. This is in direct opposition to the statements of those men who have seed to sell, but it is a fact. And, lastly, trees planted out in the open field will not be bitten by stock (in inclosures they will be ruined.)

Prospects of Pecan Culture.

I have now about a thousand trees in all. In an open, cultivated field they make a beautiful oval growth, and when not too close together no tree can surpass them in symmetry. The price for fine Pecans has not declined in the last nine years; if anything, it has advanced, for it is impossible to get the finer grades for less than $1.00 a pound, while some men charge as high as $3.00 a pound for them. Of course, when large quantities are placed upon the market the price will fall, but even at ten cents a pound they will pay much better than anything else that can be grown on the land. For many years after my grove comes into bearing there will be a large demand for the finest grade of Louisiana soft-shell Pecans for planting, and these will bring very high prices. When I begin selling them for eating purposes I shall have to be satisfied with much lower prices.

A few years ago I wrote an article on Pecan culture in which my name and address were given, and which was copied by the agricultural press. I received hundreds of letters in regard to the matter from all over the country (one coming from far-off Australia), and I might have sold $500 worth of Pecans from this article alone. Let me say here that I have neither trees nor nuts to sell just now, nor am I an agent for any one, so it will be needless to write to me. I shall not have the time to answer the letters.

A Pecan grove in bearing has several advantages over an ordinary crop. The product will sell for a great deal more than any other crop on the given land. The trees will not be injured by an overflow from the Mississippi River, the great curse of our land. They will not require any cultivation after the land is sown to clover.

I wish to draw the attention of the reader to the great superiority of the Louisiana soft-shell Pecan over the largest nuts grown in Texas. Any one who will buy a few of each kind and compare them will find that the Louisiana nuts are larger, the shells are thinner, the meat is richer, and the Pecans are of a more regular, even shape. The average Texan will be disposed to deny this fact, but it is a fact that can be proved by comparison. I have had Pecans sent me from all portions of Texas (their brag nuts), and they did not compare with the best grade of Louisiana soft-shell Pecans.

4, 9, '94.

From Catalogue of Richard Frotscher, N. O., La.

MR. RICHARD FROTSCHER, New Orleans.

DEAR SIR:—There being, as you say, "an evident desire among many here to learn something more about Pecan growing with a view of planting," I send you my views on the subject. While not professing to be a teacher, I think, if you conclude to publish this in your *Garden Manual*, it may be of interest to some who are about starting in the business; being only a plain statement of facts, without much speculation as to how profitable it may prove to those engaged in it.

It is surprising that this matter should have received so little attention up to this time, the demand for good nuts being practically unlimited.

The trees, as far as my observation goes, are subject to no disease, and have but few insect pests to contend with. They will grow in almost any soil, on high or low land, no cultivation, no draining, no pruning required. The reverse of all this true of the Orange; yet how many have spent much money in trying to establish Orange groves, and so few to plant Pecan trees. The returns from the first so uncertain, from the last absolutely sure. An Orange grove in this State may be, and often is, killed out in one night by cold, while a Pecan grove will continue to be profitable for years; for so long, in fact, that it is not even remembered who planted it.

The Pecan nut tree, *Carya Olivea Formis*, grows wild in many of the Southern States, and is said "to be indigenous along the Mississippi river as far north as Southern Iowa."

The bulk of the nuts on the market are from wild, self-sown trees. Prices vary from five cents to fifty cents per pound, showing conclusively there is a great difference in quality. The rich, sweet, oily nuts of thin shell and large size are the best. I have some now before me, some small ones seven-eighths of an inch long by three-eighths of an inch in diameter, and others one and one-eighth inch in diameter by two and one-eighth inches long. These last are ten times the value of the first, because of superior quality, thin shell and large size. These nuts are all from self-sown trees. The yield from full grown trees varies from one to seven barrels, weighing about one hundred pounds per barrel.

In no other class of wild fruit or nut trees is there a greater chance for improvement, or rather so great an improvement so easily effected. We have only to select the best sorts nature has provided and bud or graft them on the common kinds.

The most successful method is by "annular budding." It may be done any time from the end of May up to the first part of August, varying as seasons and the localities differ; the earlier it can be done the better.

With a sharp budding knife make two cuts completely around the stock, about one inch apart; cut only through the bark; cut from the top circle to the lower one a straight cut down; now slip off from the stock this piece of bark which is to be used as a pattern; that is, place it around the scion (or piece of branch on which are the buds you wish to use), covering a well developed eye; make the same cut as before on the scion, throw the first piece of bark away, fit the last piece from the scion to its place on the stock, wrap firmly (leaving the eye uncovered) with wax cotton, bass, or like soft material. To have the buds fit well the scion should be as large or larger than the stock. If the operation is well done, the buds will start in about fifteen days. When the buds have taken well take off the ties and cut back the stock to within six inches of the bud. When they have grown out a foot or more, cut back again to within a half inch of the bud. Thereafter allow nothing but the bud to grow. Pecan trees may be grafted in the ordinary way, but I have never succeeded in budding them by the common method.

Budding or grafting will cause the trees to come into bearing much earlier than from seed, to produce more regular and more abundant crops, besides perpetuating the improved kinds, which is the most important, as they do not always come true from seed.

Pecan seed should be transplanted soon after the leaves fall; it must be done before they start growing in the Spring. As they grow to be large trees, they must be planted from fifty to seventy feet apart, though on sandy poor land they may be planted closer. Keep down the weeds from around the young trees for the first year or two; afterwards they will take care of themselves.

In looking over my letter in your "Garden Manual," it struck me that I would like to say a few words more to those desirous of planting a grove of seedlings, if you think it worth while to make room for it. I wish to impress them with the importance of planting only the very best and finest nuts obtainable; to bear in mind the fact that the tendency of such seedlings is not toward an improvement on, but towards a kind inferior to the parent tree; that some only, even of the best selected nuts, reproduce their kind (it is said about sixty per cent. of the seedlings from good nuts produce good fruit); that there is no way to select the best of such seedlings but by waiting until they fruit, which may be eight to fifteen years.

Now, as there are many advertisements of "Large Soft-shelled Pecans" for sale for seed, I would advise all buyers to be very particular as to the source from whence they get their nuts for planting, otherwise they will certainly be disappointed in results, and incur an irreparable loss of years of time.

The tendency of this tree to sport or produce varieties is amply proven by the numberless kinds we now have. I have never seen two trees in a grove produce nuts exactly alike in size, shape and quality. Where it is possible to get nuts from a tree growing at some distance from others (the further the better) such nuts would certainly be the best to plant. The chances that they would reproduce this kind are greater, because the pollen from other trees would not be so likely to reach it at the time of flowering. In this connection, and while I think of it, I certainly advise any one against buying seedling trees, unless from a responsible and reliable nurseryman. There are thousands of such trees being offered for sale, professedly grown from good Pecan, but I know of barrels of almost worthless Pecans to have been sown ostensibly to make stocks for budding, but doubtless many thousands of these will be sold to supply the demand for cheap trees. Far better to plant a nut of good quality which you can see before it goes into the ground, and wait one year longer, than to plant such trees, even if they cost nothing.

It is best to raise trees in nursery before planting in orchard. Plant the nuts in rows three or four feet apart, drop the nuts in the row, sow four inches from each other, cover two inches deep, and keep the ground clear of weeds and grass. The seed may be planted any time after the nuts ripen until growth starts in the Spring. When two years old the seedlings may be easily and safely transplanted to the orchard. In my opinion, the transplanting of the tree while young is advantageous, inasmuch as it causes them to make a more spreading head, and to come earlier into bearing.

In adopting for propagation the three kinds which, on our joint investigation we concluded to be the best, I have named them the "Frotscher," "Rome" and "Centennial." As you know, they are phenomenal in size, thin shell, of rich, sweet quality and finest flavor.

That you have made a long step towards improvement by selecting only such nuts as these for seed cannot be disputed; but as they do not always come true from seed, perpetuating the good kinds can best be done by budding or grafting. This you know better than myself.

Respectfully,
WM. NELSON.

RAISING PECANS IN TEXAS.

A PROFITABLE INDUSTRY SUITED TO THE ARID REGIONS OF THAT STATE.

From the Irrigation Age.

After careful investigation in 1886 I bought land for Pecan culture on Pecan Bayou, in Texas, where I found the tree growing in its native state. I have now an orchard of eleven thousand trees on my four hundred acres that are one to six years old. As nut culture is attracting attention in the arid region, and the Pecan should thrive wherever the English Walnut does, my experience may be of interest.

The Pecan tree is valuable for its timber as well as for its nuts. Axe and hoe handles, gun stocks, furniture and various other useful articles are made from the wood. The nut, besides being used as dessert, is made into cakes and candies, and its oil brings the highest price in the market from clockmakers, gunsmiths, etc. The tree is of slow growth and long lived, one on my place being over one hundred years old in its wild state. The tree grows to the height of eighty or more feet, and its home is in the rich alluvial valleys, and will not succeed where the soil is not rich and deep.

There are two distinct varieties known as the soft and hard shell. The best among the soft shell varieties are known as the Swinden and Stuart. The wild varieties are hard shelled.

I have nearly eleven thousand trees on my four hundred acres, planted forty feet apart each way. As there is no enterprise but has its drawbacks, I must say I had them to begin with—the first thing being the wood louse or ant, which attacked the yellow pine stake placed by every nut. They then went from the stake to the tree, and thus killed the young stem; but this was obviated by cypress boxes, eighteen inches high, tarred at the bottom, which also served the purpose of protecting the young tree from the depredations of the rabbits and other rodents, which did me considerable damage. Squirrels will unearth the nuts when planted, and rabbits will gnaw the bark and cut off the tender sprouts.

The tree will come into bearing in eight to ten years. A tree at that age will produce one bushel or forty-two pounds, and sell readily at $5. At fifteen to twenty years the yield will be ten bushels or more to the tree. I have seen trees produce as high as forty bushels, and I have paid $150 for the product of one tree. Thus we can readily draw the conclusion that the profits of the Pecan will soon rival that of the famous Florida and California Orange groves. The price of Pecans varies with quality and size. The small wild ones are sometimes less than $2, while the extra large ones are in demand at as high as $8. There is no fear of glutting the market with these extra sizes, as few are willing to wait until they come into bearing. There is no safer life insurance than a well established Pecan Orchard. There are men to-day deriving a good living from a few trees planted by them, and others I know of who are getting from $3,000 to $5,000 per year from trees planted by their fathers. The land between the trees need not lie idle while the trees are coming into bearing, but can be planted to hoed crops and made to pay. I have netted on an average over $1,500 per year for the past six years from my land. I advise no one to plant in localities where there is too much rain, as the pollen is liable to be washed away, and thus keep the tree from fructifying and making fruit.

PECANS AND THEIR CULTURE.

From South Florida Home.

We make the following extracts from an exhaustive article on Pecans and their culture, in The *Texas Farm and Ranch*, by E. E. Risien, San Saba, Tex.

Planting Seed Pecans.

If we are quite sure nothing will bother them, the latter part of December is a splendid time to plant in the open ground. A spade, garden fork, shovel or hoe, in fact anything that will make a hole finger length deep will do for the planter. Plant three in a place, rake the dirt back and tramp on them; rake up some more dirt and tramp again. It is a mistake to dig large holes or bore first with a post auger, as some writers advise, so that the tap root may go down easily. Young Pecan trees don't do much good till the tap root does strike the hard dirt. A surer plan than to plant in the open ground as early as December is to bury the seed Pecans in sand in a shady place, keep wet, and let them freeze; about the first of March, or as soon as you see they have commenced bursting, plant them in a permanent place. Look out for the ants or they will make short work of them after they have bursted.

Transplanting the Pecan.

Although I cannot recommend the transplanting of the Pecan, on account of the immense tap root, yet it can be done with perfect safety, provided an abundance of water is applied. As in the case of irrigation or low lands, if a third or even more of the tap root is cut off, it is just as good, provided plenty of water is turned on. In very low land the tap root rots off any way. I had some Pecans sent me from Florida that grew on a tree that the party said had been transplanted three times. His opinion was that the fruit had improved with each tranplanting.

Yield of Pecan Trees.

The greatest yield at one time from a single tree that came under my notice was from a tree growing on the Widow Barnett place, four miles above the town of San Saba. Twenty-two bushels and a peck was measured, and the parties who did the flailing said they left fully three bushels on the tree, not being able to reach them. Five to fifteen bushels, however, are common yields per single tree, in choice locations. Fifty dollars a year, for three successive years, was the price Mr. Post, of Milburn, got for the nuts of a single tree growing on his place. Five, seven, and nine nuts growing in a single cluster are also very common, although I have counted as high as eleven. I relate these facts simply to show the possibilities of Pecan culture.

Squirrels.

We are here confronted with the most industrious pest we have to contend with. If we are as industrious in doing our work as they are in undoing it, we will make the Pecan business a success. A good shot gun is the best thing to dispose of them with, and the meat of Pecan-fed squirrels is excellent eating. Their number is also decreased by the use of common steel traps, baited with pieces of Pecan. But we cannot trust to shot guns and steel traps alone. Opossoms and coons also put many Pecans out of sight; so to effectually prohibit all intruders from going up trees, I nail a tin guard around. Old coal oil cans, having tops and bottoms taken out, and one side opened, make a cheap and desirable protection. If a tree is much stooped, then put an extra layer of tin on the upper side. Of course notice that no other trees are near enough for them to jump from on to the one so protected. Squirrels will also grabble up the Pecan nuts during the first year of planting, and in whatever state they find it. These they have an acute sense of smelling. In the first year's growth if the nut is severed from the seedling tree it will dwindle, and sometimes die."

PECANS A PROFITABLE CROP.

By I. G. Golding, Hunt Co., Texas.

It is not generally known in the North that there are Pecan orchards and groves in Texas of two hundred to four hundred acres. The nuts are used for dessert and also made into cakes, candies and oil. Of all the nut family the Pecan is by far the most valuable. The nuts possess a rich, oily meat, have a most delicious flavor, and once tasted are always sought after. A Pecan orchard is better than a gold mine or stock in any bank. From fifty to one hundred trees are set per acre, which, when in full bearing, yield four to six bushels per tree. The nuts sell at wholesale at $3 to $4 per bushel, and retail for a great deal more. Pecan culture is certainly a bonanza, and there is nothing that will give such large returns for so little labor. This paying industry has been long neglected. The nuts are as salable as flour or meat, and one hundred times the quantity now raised might be easily disposed of. The nuts are now generally sold a year in advance. Buyers contract one year for the next year's crop, agreeing to take all the nuts of an orchard at a stated price per bushel. In the Fall the nuts ripen and fall to the ground, are then raked into heaps with what is called a sweep. They are then packed in boxes or barrels for market. This work is often done by the buyer, and all the owner of the orchard or grove has to do is to see that he gets correct measure and receives the cash.

The Pecan tree is a native of the South, but hardy varieties will thrive farther North. They thrive on almost any kind of soil. All that is necessary to insure success in Pecan culture in any section of the country is to plant nuts or trees of the best early bearing and prolific varieties that are adapted to the locality where planted. Some kinds, such as the lowland bottoms species, are not suited to many parts of the country as well as some very slow-growing and scrubby varieties. Some of the best and largest yielding prolific and early bearing varieties are adapted to all parts of the United States. Seed nuts for planting, of the fine, high grade, selected and improved varieties, are sold at $3 $4 per pound; trees of the best varieties are sold rather high by nurserymen, usually seventy-five cents to $1 each. It pays to get the best. The best and cheapest way to put out an orchard or grove is to grow the trees from nuts. A few pounds of nuts will grow trees enough to supply a whole neighborhood. Growing the trees for sale is also a most profitable business, owing to their great and constantly increasing demand.

PECANS IN TENNESSEE.

By George McReill, Henry county, Tennessee, in Southern Florist and Gardener.

We live on a place in Henry county, Tennessee, called the "Old Palmer Homestead." In 1861 my father-in-law, the late E. M. Palmer, received some Pecan nuts from a son in Texas. They were so large and fine he was induced to plant a few, from which only one tree grew and bore its first crop in 1872. The nuts from this tree were fully equal to the original. The tree has produced a good crop every year since, except in 1894. Last year, 1895, the crop from this one tree weighed one hundred and sixty-five pounds, which sold readily to grocers for ten cents per pound. The 1893 crop was the largest ever gathered, weighing three hundred and forty-two and one-half pounds, which includes only the nuts sold. Some were kept for home use and we gave a good many to friends. The tree was a beautiful sight in 1893, many limbs being bent to the ground. Trunk of tree now measures two feet and four inches in diameter.

PECANS.

E. T. K., Morriston, Miss.

I have some old fields that I have quit cultivating and think of planting in Pecans. The land has been in cultivation for many years, most of it poor; the best of it would make about ten bushels of corn per acre; soil rather sandy. When is the best time to plant and how deep should the nuts be planted? How many will it take to plant twenty acres? Is it best to plant the nuts or procure young trees from a nursery?

ANSWER.—Your poor worn out field would be a long time growing a profitable crop of Pecans. The latter require a good soil in order to produce large, vigorous and productive trees. However, by manuring the soil for several feet around each young tree you may plant at once, and bring up the remainder by pea crop, etc.

It is best to plant choice nuts where you wish the trees to grow. Keep the fresh gathered nuts in a box of loose soil, buried in the ground, protected from mice, until the nuts commence to sprout in March. Then plant them in well fertilized holes thirty feet apart each way, covering about two inches deep with light soil, preferably leaf mould.

Plant the land in cow peas and fertilize with two hundred pounds acid phosphate per acre. Convert the vines into hay when in full bloom. Next year plant in cotton and manure well. Don't plant in small grain *for a crop of grain, nor in corn*. If convenient for shipping you might plant a row of Peach trees between the rows of Pecans, one way; or a row of grape vines; in either case to be removed in five or six years. One bushel of sound nuts will probably be sufficient to plant twenty acres.

PECAN ACREAGE IN FLORIDA.

From Practical Nurseryman.

Pecan growing in Florida has become in some parts an established industry, from which large returns are expected as the years go by. It is stated by the South Florida *Home* that there are now cultivated in that State about four thousand seven hundred and sixty-nine acres of Pecans, comprising one hundred and three thousand four hundred and sixty-three bearing trees. The number of trees not yet of bearing age is given at one hundred and twenty-five thousand three hundred and seventy-three. Santa Rosa county shows a large part of the cultivated groves, the acreage reported being three thousand and forty-six acres with seventy thousand three hundred and fifty-two bearing trees and seventy-five thousand seven hundred and fifty-six non-bearing trees. Citrus county has seven hundred and sixty acres in Pecans, comprising thirty-six thousand four hundred and eighty trees, and Volusia county scores one hundred and eighty-six acres and six thousand and seventy-two trees.

GRAFTING PECANS.

From Rural New Yorker.

C. E. P., OCEAN SPRINGS, MISS.—O. P., of Beverly, N. J., would like to get points on Pecan or Hickory grafting. To graft large trees is not feasible; I have tried it for years, but budding is a success, though I succeeded only last year so as to make a business of Pecan budding and grafting. About sixty per cent. of buds and grafts took well this year. Grafts can only be put into the ground, but buds will take under proper conditions in trees of any size. Buds I put in August, 1892, have made a growth of five feet and more, and are from one to two inches in diameter; even on one two Pecans are growing, which will mature perfectly. These buds were from a bearing tree. In the course of time I expect to change all my bearing trees by budding.

Several years ago I had a little controversy with W. R. Stuart, in regard to his statement that he had Pecan nuts which would produce true to seed. To-day, in all of his published articles, he advises the public to plant the nuts and afterwards graft or bud the young trees. I have worked seven years to make a success of budding or grafting, and only succeeded last year to my satisfaction. Most of my trees are nine years old, and it will be no small job to change nearly one hundred, but I have to do it if I ever expect a fair revenue from them; twenty-seven are crown-budded already, and have made a fair growth.

PECAN RAISING.

By Samuel Miller Bluffton, Mo., in American Farm and Horticulturist.

This nut is of late receiving much attention, and deservedly so, as it is among the best. There are many varieties as to size and quality, as also thinness of shell. But the most important feature about it to the beginner is how to raise them. I have never had any difficulty in this where the nuts had been properly treated; that is, to not let them get too dry. I once bought a bushel of extra large ones from the North here (as the Southern ones are too tender for our climate), packed them in sand in a box six inches deep, and set it on the ground where no water could settle around the box. They were so packed that sand was around every one. In the Spring, when the ground dried off and weather warm, I found them cracking the shell, and showing the starting germ; planted out in nursery rows six inches apart, rows four feet apart; covered the nuts about an inch deep. I don't think five per cent. failed. When one Summer's growth the tops were from three to twelve inches high, while the roots averaged eighteen inches, one tap-root being the rule. These were disposed of, and their success proved that the idea of their uncertainty of growth is a mistake. The idea of this nut not vegetating after becoming dry is a mistake, as a friend of mine told me he had succeeded twice with them by planting two inches deep, in first part of June. This was a surprise to me. The singular part of it is, he had repeatedly failed when planting them in the Fall. One important thing is to get them set where they are to remain as early as possible, as they are troublesome to transplant when a few years old.

PECANS AND ENGLISH WALNUTS.

From Southern Cultivator and Dixie Farmer.

Dr. N. F. Howard, in the Dahlonega (Ga.) *Signal*, presents the following views on the culture of Pecans and English Walnuts:

Pecans and English Walnuts do well on any lands that the Black Walnut and Hickory nut trees grow on.

As is known, on a large per cent. of the land in Lumpkin county, as well as throughout Georgia, these trees grow finely and fruit abundantly, especially when cultivated. So will the Pecan and English Walnut trees grow rapidly and bear at an early age, when properly cultivated upon a gray or red soil, with a red or dark clay foundation; or on a deep, rich, black soil, they do well. But on a poor land, with a white clay foundation, they will not thrive. The English Walnut will die out, and the Pecan will do but little good on this white clay foundation.

Six years ago I decided that it would be nice to have a Pecan orchard, and planted eight hundred nuts. Of these three hundred came up and grew. I planted thin and hard shell nuts, as purchased in the market. After this I concluded to plant only select varieties.

In November and December of 1892, and January and February, '93, I planted three hundred and eighty-two Pecans and one hundred and fifty English Walnuts, most of them by the use of dynamite. The trees set thirty-six feet each way, being thirty-four to the acre. With a slate auger a hole was bored thirty to thirty-six inches deep, and one-sixth of a pound of dynamite was used, when a hole would be blown out some forty inches deep, which was cleaned out and filled up with top soil, and the tree or nut planted in this. Rich top soil is better to fill the hole with than hot compost fertilizers. When the soil is deep and rich, the hole may not be cleaned out at all, as the ground is shivered and loosened up some forty inches deep.

I transplanted trees one, two and four years old. Also over one hundred nuts in the hill where they were to remain.

The younger the tree the better. It ought not to be more than one year old when transplanted. It is still better to plant the nut in the hill where it is to remain.

Mr. Herbert Post says the Pecan ought not to be transplanted, but the nut should be planted where the tree is to remain and grow. I am inclined to agree with him. He also states that where dynamite is used, the tree will be as large at six years as it would be at ten if planted the ordinary way, and will begin to bear fruit when six years old, and be profitable at the age of ten years. Only about one in twelve of the trees died, and about one in ten of the nuts planted in the hills failed to come up. If you want an orchard of three hundred Pecan trees, you should plant one hundred each year for three years, and then you would have a crop every year. As some trees will not bear each year, others would.

Nuts should not be planted more than three inches deep. If the planting is delayed until February, which is a very good time to plant, the nuts should be soaked in water eight or ten days so as to soften the shell before planting.

We wish to add that the demand for fruits and nuts cannot be supplied by a great deal, therefore we need not have any fears of glutting the market. No, not for generations to come. An orchard of Pecans of one thousand trees, say twenty years old, in our opinion, would yield more clear profit than any cotton farm in North Georgia.

Be sure, if you set an orchard, to secure large size, thin shell nuts, and plant on good strong land, and then cultivate them as well or better than you do an apple tree. When planted thirty-six or forty feet apart, the land will yield the crops as it has done heretofore, and in ten years the trees will bear nuts to profit. The land can then be set in clover and grasses. So there can be no loss to the owner.

THE PECAN IN MISSOURI.

S. Miller, Montgomery County, Mo.

That there are valuable varieties of this nut in the North we can testify from observation and experience. Those from Texas and Louisiana have been tried here and found tender; but we have them here of a large size and of excellent quality. Trees grown to an enormous size, near one hundred feet high, and over two feet in diameter, are common on our Missouri bottoms; and a grove of fifty tree, which the pioneer had sense enough to let stand, is a very profitable piece of land.

I know of one such about six miles from here, from which the owner realized more money one year than from the rest of his farm. I paid him eight dollars for part of the yield of one tree that season. The trees are scattered over several acres, and he farms the land nearly the same as that which is clear—raises wheat and corn. To go through this Pecan orchard and examine the difference in the nuts was quite a treat and curiosity. There are not any two exactly alike; some long and thin, pointed at both ends, others short and nearly round. The surface of some is rough, while others are quite smooth. The same difference is found in their flavor, and the amount of meat and quality of what is in the shell. Some shells are pretty hard, with thick lining partitions, while others are so thin that they can be crushed with the hand. Those large ones that I bought were packed in sand in a box with holes in th bottom for drainage, let stand on the ground out doors all winter, and in the spring, just as they began to sprout, were planted out in a row three inches apart, covered one inch deep.

I don't believe three per cent. failed. They were in good soil and made tops of from six inches to one foot. But when I got to digging them, something was learned. Many of them had roots twenty inches long, and to get them out entirely was no small job. The idea that nut trees are very difficult to transplant is erroneous; the only trouble is, persons don't do it right. I raised of that lot alluded to about one thousand, all of which were sent out all over the Union. In all my observations I have never found one on upland. River and creek bottoms are their home. An impression generally prevails that this class of nuts must be planted before they get dry, or of any age; but this is wrong, so far as the hickory is concerned, for a few years ago I planted some paper-shell hickory nuts that had lain in a drawer for three years. They were planted in the fall and every one grew. But they grew very slowly in the first two years, and it is not likely that I will ever see them bear nuts. There are thousands of acres in the South, the land of which is not used for farming, that would become very valuable in course of time if planted with the best Pecans, or planted with any good growing ones, and when ten years old grafted with the best varieties. W. R. Stuart, of Ocean Springs, Mississippi, sent me the finest yet received. On my grounds here are growing grafts of Nussbaumer's hybrid Pecan, grafted on common hickory, several feet above ground. They have not yet borne fruit, but may soon. While difficult to grow when grafted on trees of some size (and it must be crown grafting), they take readily when set on young trees a few inches under ground. Several of these hybrids or crosses, whichever they may be called, have been sent to me; and I find that several of them are larger than any Pecan I ever had seen.

PECANS IN KANSAS.

D. W. Cozad, La Cygne, Kansas, writes, November 7, 1895: I gathered over twenty-five bushels of Pecans from my young trees this season, some trees six inches in diameter producing nearly two bushels of nuts. My neighbor gathered over twenty bushels from his young trees. Many trees three to four inches in diameter were loaded. Over three hundred bushels of Pecans were gathered this season in this vicinity. In a previous communication, Mr. Cozad wrote they frequently had the thermometer several degrees below zero.

ENEMIES OF THE PECAN.

From Nut Culture in the United States, by the Department of Agriculture.

The principal enemies of the Pecan tree, in order of their importance, are exposure to light, water-soaked soil, insects, vermin, and disease. A correspondent in Texas says the Guadalupe river bottom is full of Pecan trees of all ages and in all stages of destruction, by an excess of water backed up into the soil, occasioned by the choking of the drainage channels. The wood lice get into young trees under the forks of the roots, and gradually check or destroy their growth. Caterpillars consume their foliage at times to such an extent as to destroy the crop. Worms get into the young fruit and the "Sawyer" beetle cuts off trees and branches of considerable size. All of these pests, as well as crows and vermin and Pecan diseases, are more abundant in the bottoms than the uplands. After the nuts are formed, and while their stems are still tender, an undescribed insect is reported in Texas as cutting large quantities from the trees. So far as is yet determined, the nutlets do not contain the larvæ of this insect; nor are the young nuts eaten, but the stems are cut and the nuts fall to the ground. In the latter part of May of some years, the terminal buds and tender growth of nursery stock and orchard trees are much damaged in that State by a "minute worm," which is thought by growers to be the larvæ of a fly which infests the trees. These flies are in turn kept in check by numerous small spiders which prey upon them.

Experimenters report that so far as they have tried the arsenical poisons they seem to damage Pecan trees. In California, Pecan trees have been attacked and greatly damaged by the cotton cushion scale of the Orange, but the Australian ladybird, imported for destroying the Orange insect, has cleaned up the Pecan trees as perfectly as it saved the Orange trees.

For the various caterpillars, web-worms, &c., a spraying of Paris green or London purple is recommended, and for the twig-girdlers gather and burn the twigs as they fall.

Varieties

The following are among the varieties described in "Nut Culture in the United States."

Centennial. — From *Richard Frotscher*, New Orleans, La. A large, oblong nut; thickness of shell medium; kernel plump, oily, good.

Faust.—From *O. D. Faust*, Bamberg, S. C. A long, quite large nut; valuable.

Frotscher.—From *Richard Frotscher*, New Orleans, La. Large size, thin shell, good quality.

Jewett.—From *W. R. Stuart,* Ocean Springs, Miss. A large, oblong nut, somewhat angular; shell medium thickness; quality very good.

McCallister.—From *O. L. McCallister*, Mt. Vernon, Ind. This is probably a hybrid. It is the largest nut among all the Hickories received at the office. The kernel of a well-filled specimen is in color, consistency and flavor more like a Shellbark of high quality than a Pecan.

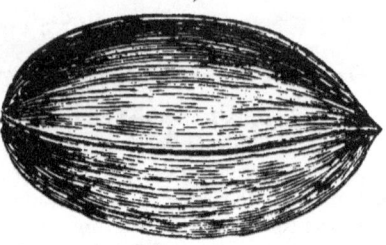

FROTSCHER.

Stuart.—From *W. R. Stuart*, Ocean Springs, Miss. One of the largest Pecans, thirty-five nuts to the pound; ovoid in form; shell very thin; kernel plump; quality good.

Van Deman.—From *W. R. Stuart,* Ocean Springs, Miss. A large nut; forty-five weigh a pound; oblong in form; shell very thin; flavor excellent.

SHELLBARKS.

The name Shellbark is given this species of the Hickory from the peculiar formation of rough shaggy bark which peels off in strips as the tree advances in age. The nuts are also encased in very heavy hulls. It is a native over the larger part of the United States extending farther North than the Pecan.

There has been but little accomplished in the improvement of Shellbark or perpetuating the superior varieties discovered, on account of their great variation when grown from seed and the difficulty with which they are propagated by budding and grafting.

The kernels of the Shellbark are largely used by confectioners and a very large trade is done in the kernels, an important feature of the nut being their "cracking quality."

William Bartram gives the following in his account of travels, published 1791: "They are held in great estimation with the present generation of Indians, particularly *Juglans Exaltata*, commonly called shell barked Hickory; the Creeks store up the latter in their towns. I have seen above one hundred bushels of these nuts belonging to one family. They pound them to pieces, and then cast them into boiling water, which after passing through fine strainers preserves the most oily part of the liquid; this they call a name which signifies "Hickory milk." It is as sweet and rich as fresh cream, and is an ingredient in most of their cookery, especially in hominy and corn cake."

A TEATIRSE ON NUT CULTURE. 119

Grafting • The same methods of grafting as employed with the Pecan are used with the Shellbark and with about the same success.

Varieties As yet but few varieties of Shellbark have been dignified with a name; probably the first to be named was

Hales' Paper Shell.—So named by the late A. S. Fuller. It originated on the farm of *Mr. Henry Hales*, of Ridgewood, New Jersey, and is probably over one hundred years old; about seventy-five feet high and nearly two feet in diameter; nut very large; shell very thin—in fact, much thinner than many Pecans that come to the Northern markets; kernels full, plump, rich and delicious, with the rare feature of retaining their excellent quality for two or more years without becoming rancid. A very valuable variety.

Jackson.—From *J. F. Rice*, Berlin Cross Roads, Ohio. A large, smooth, compressed, oval nut, with moderately thin shell, and large plump meat; excellent quality.

Leaming.—From *R. G. Leaming*, Sedalia, Missouri. A large nut of fine flavor and very good cracking qualities, the meat coming out freely in uninjured halves.

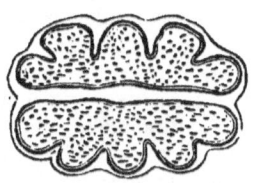

HALES' PAPER SHELL.

Other Hickories There are a number of other species of the Hickory— Mocker Nut, Pig Nut, Nutmeg Hickory, Bitternut, Water Hickory—all of which are thick-shelled and of little value commercially.

WALNUTS—(*Juglans.*)

Of the *Walnuts* of commercial value in the United States there are the Black Walnut (*Juglans Nigra*), and the Butternut (*Juglans Cinerea*), which are natives of this country.

The Persian Walnut (*Juglans Regia*), and the Japanese Walnuts.

Native Walnuts. The Black Walnut and Butternut have not been grown in orchard form to any extent, though they have been planted extensively for timber purposes.

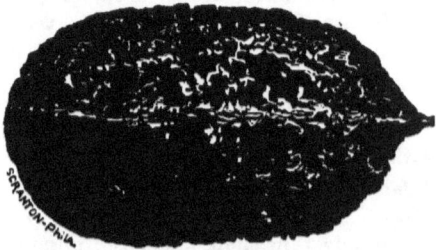

BUTTERNUT.

Tree, when standing alone, with room to develop, makes a large, spreading, handsome tree, with odd, pinnate leaves; leaflets from fifteen to twenty-one, mainly oblong and pointed; male and female flowers on the same tree; fruit, round or oblong; husk, thin, drying up with opening the husk; shell, rough and thick; kernel, fleshy, rich and oily. They are found pretty generally throughout the United States, except the Gulf and Southern Atlantic Coast, preferring low, moist, rich, loamy ground.

Propagation

There have been but few attempts to propagate any distinct varieties of Black Walnut or Butternut by budding or grafting, as there appears to be less variation from seed than with other nuts and fruits, and but few varieties of superior qualities have been discovered.

They are used to some extent on which to graft the Persian Walnut, and the mode generally adopted is the cleft-graft, with fair success.

AMERICAN BLACK WALNUT.
GILBERT.

Gilbert.—From *H. K. Gilbert*, Columbus, N. J. Tree young, good grower; very productive; nut very large, round; shell thin; kernel full, plump and good quality.

Persian Walnut.—(*Juglans Regia.*)

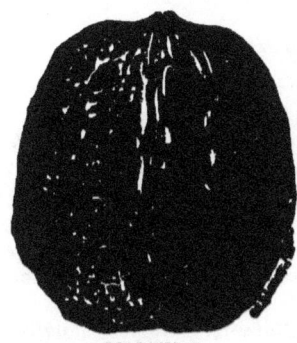
MADEIRA.

Known, commercially, as the English Walnut, Madeira nut. In America it is known as "English Walnut," to distinguish it from our native species. In England it is known as Madeira nut, probably because the nuts were formerly imported from the Madeira Islands. The tree is a native of Asia, and was introduced by the Greeks from Persia into Europe. From Greece to Rome, thence throughout Continental Europe, and finally to England, and grown extensively for its timber, which entered largely into the manufacture of gun stocks and furniture, it being susceptible of very high polish. It is reported as much as £600 was paid for a single large tree in England, to be used for gun stocks. The introduction of Black Walnut and Butternut timber very much reduced the price, and more attention was given to the nuts.

The **Persian Walnut** has been grown in the United States more than a century, and until recently the plantings were confined to the Atlantic Coast, from Massachusetts to Georgia, there being some very fine specimens in Philadelphia and New Jersey that produce good crops of very good-sized nuts.

On the Pacific Slope the conditions are more favorable, though in the northern portions, notwithstanding the tree makes good growth, it fails to produce nuts, probably on account of the bloom being imperfectly pollenized.

The **Persian Walnuts** require rich, moist, well drained ground, and are planted largely in the southern counties of California, the largest cultivated orchard being seven hundred acres.

Propagation   The orchards of **Persian Walnuts** have been generally on their own roots, not grafted, though in some instances the California native Walnut has been used. This, as a stock, may prove of value in the Gulf and Southern Atlantic States, where the Persian Walnuts are subject to "root knot."

They are readily propagated from seed, as previously described. By grafting, the cleft graft is the usual style.

WALNUT GROWING IN CENTRAL AND NORTHERN CALIFORNIA.

Ira W. Adams, in Pacific Rural Press.

The *Rural Press* of January 4th, 1895, if I remember rightly, contained quite a long article of mine on "Walnut Growing in Upper Napa Valley." Since that time I have read very carefully in different papers and magazines several interesting articles from other standpoints as to the growing of Walnuts in this State, and, while not agreeing with all the theories advanced by the different writers on the subject, I am satisfied it has been the means of creating an interest in what will eventually prove to be a very valuable resource to many thousands who have heretofore given but very little attention to the subject.

It is very evident to me that the growing of Walnuts is very gradually, but surely, coming to the front, not only in this favored county but in many other portions of this State, where the growing of this most excellent, nutritive and valuable nut has, up to the present time, been almost, if not quite, entirely overlooked.

I acknowledge that I am an enthusiast as to the growing of the Walnut, for in my judgment the day is not far distant when hundreds of acres of these beautiful trees will be seen growing, luxuriantly loaded with their precious fruit, not only in the broad valleys, but in the countless smaller ones, as well as the foothills and more elevated portions of Northern California, even where the snow falls to the depth of several feet.

I read a short article not long since written by a man in Southern California, who said, among other things:

The growing of the Walnut is peculiarly adapted to Southern California, and even here the area is very limited where they will thrive successfully, and, therefore, it is very evident that the growing of this nut will always be very profitable to those who are fortunate enough to own land in such highly favored localities.

I beg to differ altogether from the writer of this article. If the area there is so very limited for the successful growing of the Walnut, let the people there who wish to engage in the industry, especially those whose purses are somewhat depleted and consequently have not the means to buy the land for that purpose, come to the Northern counties of this State, where the area for Walnut growing is unlimited, and where no irrigation is needed; where there are many thousands of acres of land that can be purchased at a nominal price; where trees will flourish in all their beauty; where there is plenty of wood, living springs, pure air, and consequently a healthy climate, neither too hot in summer nor too cold in winter.

THE MATTER OF LOCAL LIMITATIONS.—It has not been many years since the successful growing of the Orange, and even the Grape, was supposed to be confined to the immediate vicinity of Los Angeles, and even the successful raising of the French Prune was supposed to be confined to a somewhat limited area in Santa Clara valley. So I predict it will be with the Walnut, and that the area for the successful raising of the same is altogether beyond the bounds of my most enthusiastic imagination. I do not believe in advocating that this or that particular county is one of the best, if not the very best, locations for growing Oranges, Prunes, Walnuts, etc. Go to work and plant what you believe will be a success in your locality, and then let the Rip Van Winkles come along and wake up with astonishment when they see what you have been doing when they were in their lethargic sleep.

RECENT LESSONS.—The past season I have learned something about Walnut growing that I consider worth a great deal to me, and I think it will be of inestimable value to those who contemplate putting out Walnut trees in the future, especially in the northern counties of this State, as well as in Oregon, Washington and Nevada. Last season, on the night of April 18th, my Prune crop was entirely destroyed when the Prunes were about three-eighths of an inch in diameter. On examining them the next morning I was completely surprised to find them frozen, something that never happened here before to my knowledge. My Walnut trees, with the exception of three, were in full leaf at this time, but the freeze not only destroyed the foliage entirely, but the ends of the young shoots that were making a very rapid growth. The sight of these large trees, with their foliage as black as though they had been swept by a severe fire, I must confess was really discouraging, as well as distressing, to me, and I mercifully desisted from looking at them as much as possible. It was a number of weeks before the new foliage started, and more than a month before the trees assumed anywhere near the condition that they were in before the fatal freeze. However, these trees bore a small crop of nuts—very much more than I expected.

LATE GROWING WALNUTS.—But one sight gladdened my eyes. On carefully examining the three other trees I found that not even a single bud had started. Two of them commenced to bud May 3d and the other some weeks later, if I remember rightly. I regret very much that I lost my memoranda as to the extreme late date of the budding of this tree, which, however, was too young to bear. One of these three trees that I have mentioned made a wonderful growth of foliage in a short time, and escaped the many severe frosts that followed the fatal freeze of April 18th, and produced over two hundred nuts, which are as large as, if not larger than, any other variety I raise. This variety of tree, bearing such large soft-shelled nuts, I consider very valuable in connection with its extreme lateness in bearing, and, if I were a young man,

I would get at it as soon as possible and set out one hundred and sixty acres or more where land is comparatively cheap. I would then have no fear of frost, but while other people were smudging their Grape vines, Prune trees, etc., in the cold midnight air, night after night, for fear of losing their crop, I would quietly lie in my warm bed and "smile at Satan's rage," owing to the fact that my late variety of Walnut trees were entirely safe.

EXPERIENCE IN SONOMA COUNTY.—I have just received a letter from J. H. Hornbeck, of Santa Rosa, in which he gives the following interesting account of his experience:

I send to-day a tin box with nine of my Santa Rosa Soft-shelled Walnuts. They are not as large as former crops, nor so fair in color—are not sulphured. I never sulphur anything. The frosts last Spring killed them nearly all—I only got two pounds from the five bearing trees. In 1895 they had about ten pounds to the tree; in 1894 about thirty pounds each. They were planted in 1885, yearling seedlings, from six inches to one foot high; have had nuts on six seasons, and now girt at six inches above ground twenty and one-half, twenty-six and one-half, twenty-six and one-half, twenty-two, twenty-seven and one-half inches, respectively. Mr. Burbank propagated them. They are in adobe soil, have had no extra care, and are but little trouble to take care of. I am in favor of high branching; do not want the first limbs of Walnut lower than seven feet. I branched my first ones about three feet high, but I think it wrong. My younger ones I will let branch higher. I have one hundred and thirty-four trees, but mostly planted the last three years. I recommend planters to fill any vacant space with Walnuts, and there seems to be quite a demand for trees. It is my opinion that the Walnut is the best tree to work with in this locality.

On reading Mr. Hornbeck's letter I was very forcibly struck with its contents, especially as to the damage to his Walnut trees by frost last season, etc. The more I think of it the more I see the propriety of planting a late variety of nuts. What we want is a variety that will be loaded with fruit when our prune crop is partially if not wholly ruined by frost. I think, as I said above, I have one Walnut tree that did not burst its buds in the least until June 2d, but am not sure, as I lost my memoranda. I shall know for certain the coming season.

I believe Mr. H. is right in branching his trees high. Mine are none less than six feet, and some eight feet or more. Still, I have had to lop off some of the limbs that otherwise would, when loaded with nuts, touch the ground.

IMPORTANCE OF THE SUBJECT.—I have written somewhat at length in this article, as I consider it of great importance to any one who expects to set out a Walnut orchard to be very careful to secure a very late variety, and thus escape heavy losses in future years from the icy king. If I had planted this or some other late variety of tree when I set out my Prune orchard, I might the past season have had a large and valuable amount of nuts to offset my total loss of prunes. Allow me to say, in conclusion, that I have been a resident of this State nearly forty-five years, and now, in my sixty-fourth year, I feel it my duty to call the attention of the many thousands who are tilling the soil for a bare living, and are anxiously looking for something more remunerative, and that will increase in value as the years roll on, to the growing of the soft-shelled Walnut.

BAY STATE GARDEN, CALISTOGA, CAL., January 14, 1897.

Mr. Adams, in his interesting letter, has overlooked mention of the fact that Felix Gillet, of Nevada City, has for the last twenty-two years, to the personal knowledge of the writer, been urging just these points upon the attention of the readers of the *Rural Press*. It was established long ago by the testimony of Mr. Gillet, W. B. West and others that the failure of the English Walnut in the upper half of the State is due to the growth of varieties not suited to the climate. The late starting of the Praeparturiens, and some other of the French varieties, has been frequently urged and fortified by many instances. Of course, these facts go to support the points which Mr. Adams draws from his experience.

THE BLACK WALNUT AND BUTTERNUT.

From Vick's Magazine.

Our native Black Walnut (*Juglans Nigra*) is amongst nuts what bacon is amongst meats, strong and greasy. The Shellbark is delicate as cream, the Pecan next in delicacy, next the English Walnut, and then our own hardy species. Its nuts are rich in oil, and might be used as English Walnuts are used in Cashmere, where one million one hundred and fifty thousand pounds of kernels are annually consigned to the oil press. Another objection to the Black Walnut is its hard shell, but the tree is very valuable as timber, and where planted for this purpose, the nuts might at least be saved to swell the sum total, for at a low price they sell readily, and are borne in heavy crops long before the trees reach "timber size." Southern boys store them away by wagons full for winter use, and disguised in nut cakes and candy they are very palatable. A "Curly Black Walnut" log of large size will sell for a fabulous price.

Juglans Cinerea, or Butternut, is not so abundant as *Juglans Nigra*, is better adapted to poor soils, colder climates and higher altitudes, is seldom planted for timber and has a nut much like the Black Walnut in flavor and quality. In shape it is very different, being long and narrow and easily cracked, splitting lengthwise in whole or half kernels. The tree bears heavily when quite young.

NUT GROWING IN SONOMA COUNTY.

By Luther Burbank, of Santa Rosa, at the Santa Rosa Farmers' Institute.

The culture of the Olive, which, here on our picturesque hills and mountains, finds its most congenial home; the Orange in our sheltered dales; the Sugar Beet, with several thousand pounds of sugar per acre, in our fertile, sunny valleys, will make the whole land smile with wealth, and add still more industries to the wonderfully varied ones of this great, and, horticulturally speaking, only half explored Sonoma county.

WALNUTS.—And still another is Walnut culture, which has been so persistently and surprisingly overlooked, probably from the fact that the few Walnuts first planted happened to be an unproductive, half wild stock, which, though growing with wonderful freedom and vigor, only occasionally produced a few inferior nuts after many years of patient waiting, but never sufficient to inspire confidence enough to induce planting for profit. But, while we have been sleeping, our Southern friends have found improved varieties, which they have planted largely, and princely incomes are now and have been received from the Southern Walnut groves.

The counties of Santa Barbara, Ventura, Los Angeles and Orange are the only ones at the present time that can be said to produce Walnuts as a commercial crop, and yet in 1894 there were five million five hundred and forty-five thousand pounds of Walnuts exported from Southern California, and this year the crop is figured at six million pounds. In the year 1894 the United States imported about fifteen million pounds of various nuts, and in the period from 1880 to 1890 not less than $7,124,575 worth, and the importation and consumption of nuts is now steadily increasing at the rate of 45 per cent. per annum.

Do the planters of Sonoma county, knowing the above facts, think the market will soon have a surplus of nuts?

Nuts are a very nutritious and inexpensive food. They supply the same hydro-carbonaceous compounds and mineral salts found in butter, bread, meat and eggs, and in a concentrated but attractive and easily digestible form.

FITTED TO SONOMA COUNTY.—The writer, some twelve years ago, was surprised to notice the finest Persian—often called English or French—Walnuts that he had ever seen, growing as far North as Shasta county. After a thorough personal investigation of the best Walnut growing sections of the State, and comparisons of growth, early bearing and productiveness of the trees, and quality of the nuts, he became convinced that Sonoma county is one of the best, if not the very best, locations in the State for Walnuts. If the right variety is planted, nuts can be produced here as early and abundantly as anywhere, and superior in plumpness and quality to any placed on the market.

Happily, the Walnut does not absolutely need grafting, as for all practical purposes the nuts very fairly reproduce themselves.

SANTA ROSA SOFTSHELL.—Many Walnut planters in this region were greatly delighted a few years ago to see their trees, only four or five years of age, bearing heavy crops of superb, large, thin-shelled Walnuts. They supposed they had the only trees of a wonderful new kind, but by comparing notes, they were all traced back to one lot of nuts from a superior tree, planted in nursery by the writer in 1885. By general consent, it has been called the Santa Rosa Softshell.

The culture of the Walnut offers the strongest inducement to planters. Few trees are required per acre, and constant pruning, thinning and spraying are not necessary. The improved varieties bear as early and more certain than prunes, and require less capital and attention. The crop is handled after the main rush of fruit harvest is over, when labor is plentiful and cheap, and, best of all, the Walnut grower is not a slave, for he can hold his crop when prices do not suit him.

HINTS ON PLANTING.—In planting Walnuts, select deep, loamy, sandy soil. The trees will not do their best unless the roots can go down several feet without meeting hardpan or other impervious obstructions. The deeper the soil the better. The trees will not need irrigation in Sonoma county, as they generally do in the South, as the meats here always fill out full and sweet, with a thin, attractive, white pelliole, without any artificial aid.

If you are unable to obtain young trees of the variety you desire, get the nuts you wish to reproduce and plant them yourself in March or April, one and a half or two inches deep on any light, rich, well-drained soil, in rows four or five feet apart, and one or two feet apart in the rows. Cultivate well for one, two or three years, then remove carefully and plant forty or fifty feet apart each way. Set the trees down as deep as they grow in the nursery.

The after culture is the same as with fruit trees, but very little pruning is necessary. At eight to twelve years of age, if all goes well, an annual crop of eight hundred to one thousand pounds per acre may reasonably be expected.

OTHER NUTS.—The Softshell Japan Walnut grows rapidly here, and yields surprising annual crops of most delicious nuts. They are at present very scarce and almost unobtainable at any price, having been lately discovered and introduced.

Among other nuts that may be profitably planted here are Butternuts, Pecans, Japanese Mammoth, Spanish and Chinese Chestnuts, as well as the native Golden Chestnuts, excellent also for ornament and shade. Others worthy of attention are Improved Almonds, Japanese Butternuts, Japanese Oak Nuts, Beechnuts, Filberts, Pistachios, and the various Hickory Nuts.

OAKS, HICKORIES AND WALNUTS.

By Joseph Meehan, in Albany Cultivator.

It is the general belief among those not practically engaged in the raising of seedlings that Acorns and Nuts must be sown in the Fall. This is but partly true. It is correct to this extent, that there must be no drying out of the seeds permitted; but with few exceptions those who raise seedlings as a business do not sow the seeds until Spring. The exceptions are among the Oaks. There are a few species which must be planted as soon as they are gathered, or within a few weeks thereafter, or they decay. These sorts are White Oak, Post Oak, and Chinquapin Oak. Many will have noticed the Acorns of these sorts lying under the trees and pushing their roots into the damp ground. On account of this habit they are always sown in the Fall very soon after they are collected.

All other Oaks and the Hickories and Walnuts are better stored away until Spring. Indeed, some of them, the Pecan nut and English Walnut, for example, will rot in the ground if sown in Autumn. The most successful men keep all seeds till Spring. The practice is to get the kinds together as soon as they are ripe, and place them in boxes or barrels mixed with almost dry earth, and keep them in some cool place till Spring. One of the most successful men I know does not even mix his seeds with soil. He has an old-fashioned barn cellar with earth floor, which is always slightly damp. His Acorns and Nuts are placed in boxes, each sort by itself, with no soil at all with them, and there they remain all winter, absorbing a little moisture instead of losing it, so that when Spring comes they are as plump as they can be, and every sound one of them grows. Keeping the kernels plump is about the whole secret of successful storing. Where such damp cellars are not available, mixing with soil or sand effects the same purpose. The material need be but slightly damp, just enough so that the seeds mixed with it do not lose weight.

The idea entertained by many, and which, in fact, has been advanced by more than one writer, that frost is necessary to the developing of nut seeds to seedlings, is not at all correct. A Hickory, Walnut and such stone seeds as Peach, Plum and Cherry, do not need frost. I think the three last named are the better for being in soil moderately damp all winter, but frost is not essential. Consideration would convince anyone that frost is not necessary, for in the Southern States, where no frosts occur, these seeds sprout as freely as they do here.

Referring again to the early sprouting acorns, I have known them to have been kept over in dryish soil until spring. But sowing them at that time is troublesome, as they have an inch or two of root then which needs careful handling.

Sowings could be made where the trees are desired, two or three seeds in a place, all but the strongest plant to be taken out in the fall. In commercial places the sowings are in narrow beds—not wider than can be reached over for the purpose of weeding. The work is done as early in spring as the season will permit. The seedlings are transplanted the next spring, or the second one thereafter, not often going to the third year.

FLORIDA FRUITS.

By Herbert Post, in South Florida Home.

The Japan Walnut.

The Japan Walnut is clearly distinct from all others, is found growing wild in the mountains of Northern Japan, and is, without doubt, as hardy as an oak. The tree grows rapidly, and attains a very large size with a magnificent spreading top. The leaves are of immense size, and of charming shade of green. The nuts, which are produced in extreme abundance, grow in clusters of fifteen to twenty in a cluster, are considerably larger than the common Hickorynut, have a shell thicker than the English Walnut, but not as thick as the Black Walnut. The meat is sweet, of the very best quality, and can be removed entire. The tree grows with great vigor, matures early, bears young, and is easily grafted on the common Walnut, yet it comes perfectly true from the seed. It is more productive than the English Walnut, and next to the Pecan it is our most reliable nut bearing tree. It has an abundance of fibrous roots and can be transplanted as safely as an Orange tree. It is adapted to Florida soil and climate, and it is surprising that it is not generally grown throughout the State.

Money in Pecan Culture.

While there may be money made in Florida in growing of Oranges, Lemons, Pineapples, &c., for which the State is well adapted, they don't begin to pay the profits that are to be obtained in the cultivation of the Texas thin shell Pecan.

Being of such a hardy nature, of same family as the Hickory and Black Walnut, the Pecan will grow in the high pine lands, sandy lands, moist lands, in fact in any land that will grow any kind of trees—not only in Florida, but every other State in the Union. No American tree known, which is so free from insect pests or disease of any kind, as the Pecan, none requires so little care, when once well under way. Beginning to bear at six years of age, at eight years they begin to bring in a handsome income and go on increasing until the trees are thirty years old and continuing for generations.

I know of no industry, or of any investment a man of small means can make, that so surely brings annual returns of large income, on so small an investment, as is obtained in this branch of aboriculture.

Thirty dollars will plant ten acres, and when the trees bear but twenty pounds each the earnings net more annually than $35,000 invested in Government bonds.

An investment of only $3.00 per acre in planting fifty acres will, when the trees bear but fifty pounds per tree, give more net earnings than $200,000 invested in a bank with eight per cent. earnings. One thousand acres in the best Pecans will, when the trees earn but $1.65 each, bring in an income exceeding $100,000 annually, which is equal to $1,000,000 in banking business earning ten per cent. annual gross.

We mention these facts to show the great value of the industry, which is so little known, and which every person with a few acres can indulge in.

Nut and fruit growing are industries which can be carried on on a large scale on business principles, and made to pay enormous incomes.

We have near here a grove of four hundred acres, planted four years ago, of the best thin-shell Pecans, containing upwards of ten thousand trees. In four years more the owner expects to have an income of at least $50,000 annually, and increase. His expectation is not an unreasonable one. Even divide that by two and it is a very comfortable income. This growing of Pecans on a large scale is not fancy farming. It is just as legitimate as any branch of farming, with vastly less risk, cost and care than any other crop. In California they diversify and grow great varieties on one tract of land, all under one management.

At Acampo, California, is a ranch of one thousand and fifteen acres, on which is now growing the following: Thirty-four thousand Almond trees, ten thousand Peach trees, eight thousand Olive, seven thousand Prune, three thousand Apricot, three thousand Fig, one thousand Pear, nine hundred Orange, five hundred Cherry, five hundred Plum and sixteen thousand of table and raisin Grapes. Although but young in bearing, the income from this ranch is enormous.

The Gulf States can grow with great profit many of the above named fruits and nuts, and make more money than can be made in California—they being so much nearer market.

A man in any of these States who will build him up industries of this kind can well afford to let the other fellow grow five-cent cotton.

It is a rare fact that any person well started in such occupations have to give a mortgage on their crop to live on while it is growing. The sooner the cotton States take up such industries the sooner will they become independent and make money. No one need fear that this generation will ever see enough

Pecans grown to become unsalable. We have the world for our market, with no competition outside the United States, as the Pecan is grown only on this continent. The term "paper shell" Pecan is misleading, and hereafter we will use the terms "thin shell" and "hard shell," as these names represent the whole.

We have seen the so-called Mexican paper-shell as thick as our hard-shell.

Never plant a Pecan tree which has had the tap root cut; if you do, you will be disappointed when the time comes for them to bear; the nut bearing of such a tree is of little or no value, but you have only a handsome and valuable shade tree worth all it cost, for that.

Experience here with our best growers has taught this lesson, and it is too expensive for others to try.

Plant the nuts only, from your own trees, and you know what you may expect in fruit—"A word to the wise," &c.

FORT WORTH, TEXAS, October, 1894.

WALNUT HULLS.

Referring to the utilization of waste material in the garden and farm, the *California Fruit Grower* has the following interesting note regarding the husks or hulls of the English Walnut: "A prominent Walnut grower of Ventura county has been requested to put a price on his Walnut husks, and is now drying a few hundred pounds for an experimental shipment. The would-be purchaser expects to use the husks for dyeing purposes. Like the husk of the Butternut and the Black Walnut, the outer covering of the California Walnut stains the hands a rich glossy brown, which is found a very fast color by the enquiring mind pursuing investigation in this avenue of research. If this waste product can be utilized for such a purpose, it will form a notable addition to that class of economic processes which reclaim waste and refuse material and adapt it to new and practical uses."

VARIETIES OF THE WALNUT IN EUROPE.

From Rural Californian.

The Walnut season is approaching, and a few remarks on their consumption in various countries may not be out of place. When about half or three parts grown, the Walnut is used for pickling. There are many varieties of these nuts, such as the oval, round, double, large and small fruited, early and late, tender thin shelled and thick shelled. An almost huskless variety occurs in the north of China.

Walnuts always command a ready sale at markets in large towns, where, at the first coming in September, they are brought in their husks and sold by the sack or bushel; but afterwards, cleared of the outer husk, they are sold both by measure and by the thousand. The larger portion of the Walnuts consumed in England are of foreign growth, and average in quantity about two hundred and fifty thousand bushels. The bulk of these come from France and Belgium, and small quantities from Germany, Holland and Italy.

The aggregate exports from Bordeaux are about sixty-five thousand hundred weight yearly. Small quantities find their way from Chili to Europe. Walnuts are a notable production of Perigord, in France, the annual product there being estimated at £40,000 in value. The best, which are large, are called "Marrons," come from the Canton of Luc, in Provence. To obtain first-class fruit the tree is grafted in France.

The culture of the common Walnut (*Juglans regia*) is diffused all over Italy, from the Alpine to the Sicilian valleys; however, the number of these trees has lately somewhat diminished, on account of the incessant demand for its timber, which is much used in carpentery—but in general, the tree is more valued on account of its fruit. When the nuts are fully ripe, which is in September and October, the kernel, deprived of its investment skin, is eaten in great quantities. As long as the skin can be easily removed, they are a nutritious and healthy article of diet, but when they get dry, so that the adhering skin sticks to them, they become indigestible.

Walnuts in the shell yield about one-third their weight of picked kernels, which are the crumpled cotyledons or seed leaves. In some northern districts, particularly in Piedmont, the Walnut tree has always been held in high estimation for the production of oil, which, when newly made, has a very agreeable taste, and can be employed in cookery, as well as in the preparation of varnish.

The Canadian Walnut, although double the size of the English Walnut, contains a much smaller kernel, with a different flavor, being strong and slightly pungent. The seeds of the Black Walnut of North America (*J. nigra*) are more oily than those of the European Walnut. A large tree will yield fifteen to twenty bushels in a season, selling at four shillings per bushel.

The Butternut, or Grey Walnut of America (*J. cinerea*) has a taste similar to the Brazil Nut. The kernel of *J. sieboldianum* of Japan has a taste like the Butternut, but less oily, and the shell is not so thick as that of the Black Walnut.

The nuts of *J. mandschuria*, allied to *J. cinerea*, are also available for the table. The kernels of the Butternut in former times were pounded by the Indians of North America and boiled; this operation separated the oily substance, which was used by them as we use butter, hence its common name.

The Persian Walnut is about a third, or a half, larger than the English

Walnut; of an elongated shape, with a very rich meat or kernel, and the shell as thin as paper. It is not an unusual thing for a tree eight to twelve years old to bear thirty thousand nuts, or one thousand two hundred pounds. There are four kinds, the Kanate, the Wanter, the Denu, and the Kaghazi, the last of which is the finest nut grown.

The Walnut grows abundantly in Kashmir, Nepal, and other parts of India, where the fruits are largely used. It forms also an important article of consumption in Japan, quantities being eaten in a raw state. They are also much used there for making a kind of confection by cracking and removing the shell, without hurting the kernel, which is afterwards coated with white sugar, thus making an attractive and agreeable sweetmeat.

The Walnut also furnishes there a bland oil, used for domestic purposes. In China it seems to be specially pressed for oil, as in some years over twelve thousand tons of Walnut pulp are exported from the port of Tientsin in the year. The Walnut is extensively cultivated in the Punjab, Himalaya, and Afghanistan, a large annual supply being brought to the plains of India by the Kabuli and other traders from the hills. The nut ripens there from July to September. There are several well known forms of this nut met with, the soft-shell kind from Kashmir and Chamba being regarded as the best. A bushel of Walnuts will yield fifteen pounds of peeled kernels, and these will produce half that weight in oil.

Hickorynuts (*Carya alba*) are very generally eaten in the United States, and are highly esteemed. It is a fine nut, peculiarly shaped, encased in a thin but strong shell. The kernel in flavor and formation resembles pretty closely that of the English Walnut. The nuts of *C. microcarpa*, closely related to *C. alba*, are of pleasant taste but smaller. Those of another species, the Shell-bark Hickory (*C. amara*), are thin-shelled, and, being exceedingly bitter, are not edible. The nut of *G. sulcata* is of a sweet, pleasant taste. The Mocker nut (*C. tomentoso*) is small but sweet and very oily. A variety produces nuts as large as a small apple, which are called King nuts. The Pecan nut (*C. Olivæformis*) is considered a delicacy superior to the common Walnut. It breaks easily, and has a nut entirely free from divisions. The nuts keep long and do not turn rancid, and are exported to the West Indies. Texas annually exports these nuts to the value of £10,000. The Pecan begins to bear at about ten years, and the yield annually increases in quantity until the full growth of the tree is attained.—P. L. SIMMONDS, F. L. S., in *The* (London) *Gardeners' Chronicle*.

The Common Walnut.

From December 12, 1896, issue of The Garden.

Walnuts Have been unusually plentiful this year, and, with a singularity which I have never hitherto observed their period of ripening has been prolonged for a length of time of which we have no previous record. The first ripe fruits made their appearance in the beginning of September, and the supply of excellent freshly gathered nuts was extended beyond the middle of October. This is a plain proof that among the plantations of ordinary Walnut trees, which are generally grown from seed and not grafted, varieties exist which differ from one another, not only in the quality of their fruit, but also (what is equally important) in their time of ripening. As I have eaten more Walnuts this year than I can remember that I have ever eaten before in all my life, I am desirous of saying a few words about this fruit.

According to Mons. Chas. Baltet, Paris alone annually consumes about six thousand eight hundred and seventy-five tons of dried Walnuts. Besides these the freshly gathered nuts are in great request at all dinner tables. These fresh nuts are better and more easily digested when eaten with a little salt. Later on, when the skin does not separate so readily from the kernel, they should be partaken of very sparingly, as not only are they then indigestible, but are apt to bring on a cough, and, with some persons, a headache. In the country there is perhaps even a larger consumption of dried Walnuts than in towns. My own opinion is that they are not so good as dried Almonds, and these, again, are not so good as Almonds in the fresh state. Walnuts are utilized in some departments of France for the manufacture of oil. In preparing this, the kernels are separated from the broken shells and the laminar partitions of the nuts. The kernels, which are found to have turned blackish or brown, are put aside to furnish lamp oil. Oil for table use is made from the others. The first drawn oil (which is obtained by pressure, without the aid of fire-heat or hot water) is termed "huile vierge." This improves by keeping and is then highly valued for certain pharmaceutical preparations. Oil of the second quality (which is extracted by the aid of heat from residuum of the first drawn oil) is termed "huile cuite," and is used for making soap and in painting; it dries very quickly, and enters into the composition of various kinds of varnishes and printing inks. Walnuts are also eaten in the green state, while the kernel is still of a milky consistence. They are then prepared by cutting them in two and leaving them to steep and soften in water mixed with vinegar. They are also pickled like Gherkins, but required to be more strongly spiced, and it is especially necessary that, when used for pickling, they should be gathered before the shells have become too hard. The right time for doing so is while the nuts can be pierced through and through in every part with a needle. In addition to these uses, Walnuts are also employed in confectionery. In Auvergne, according to M. Baltet, certain establishments for preserved fruits prepare the skinned kernels of Walnuts with sugar, making the preserve up in short-necked, wide-mouthed bottles. In Belgian Limbourg also Walnuts are sold in the green state to the confectioners. At Portiers three oil factories send out annually one hundred and thirty-two thousand gallons of Walnut oil. With the seven thousand five hundred acres of Walnut plantations on alluvial and calcareous soils, the department of Lot produces annually about eight thousand and sixty-six tons of Walnuts and employs one hundred oil-pressing machines. A Walnut tree in good bearing yields annually about one hundred and seventy-six pounds weight of nuts, and the proportion of oil which is extracted at the factories is equal to about eighteen per cent. of the weight of the nuts. The pressed residue of the nuts is used, like linseed oil cake, for feeding cattle and also as a manure. Fattening poultry, especially turkeys, by means of Walnuts, is a practice well known amongst the Walloon poultry raisers, and in country places poultry are frequently thus prepared for special family dinners or festive meetings of friends.

It is evident that from a commercial point of view the Walnut is an excellent kind of fruit, the culture of which has, perhaps, been somewhat neglected of late. Statistics show that in France the production in the year 1885 amounted to over eighty thousand tons, representing a money value of twenty-five millions of francs (£1,000,000).

The Walnut is usually propagated from seed, but, as in the case of other fruit trees properly so called, the special qualities of the parent tree are not reproduced by this mode of increase, although it may be admitted that by a careful selection of the seed parents a certain amount of constancy might be attained in the reproduction of varieties. At present, superior varieties, the fruit of which has a higher market value than the ordinary kinds, must be propagated by grafting. Grafted Walnut trees are much more productive than those raised from seed, and this forms an additional inducement to employ this mode of reproduction when local conditions create a preference for one variety more than another, either on account of the fine appearance of the fruit, the quality of the kernel, or the earliness or lateness of the time of ripening. Walnut grafting is no novelty, the practice having been recommended by Olivier de Serves about A. D. 1600, but the operation is not a very easy one, and, to be successful, requires dexterity and experience.

The methods employed are those known as pipe grafting and cleft grafting. One of the most successful ways is a modification of cleft grafting in which the scion is cut with a bificuration or fork at the lower end, into which the top of the stock is inserted, having been previously cut so as to fit exactly into the fork.*

The grafts must be well secured with ligatures and carefully covered with grafting wax or similar air-tight material.

The Walnut tree is by no means fastidious as to the soil in which it is planted, and may be seen growing in ground of the most sterile character; but, to thrive properly, it requires soil of a calcareous, schistous, or volcanic nature. It will not grow in granitic soil, and damp, clayey ground is almost equally unsuitable for it. A native of the mountains of Asia Minor and Central Asia, it was introduced into Europe at a very early period, and was already naturalized in Greece when Theophrastus wrote his "History of Plants" (B. C. 314). It seems to have been next introduced into Italy, whence it made its way into other parts of Europe. Resisting with difficulty the inclemencies of the more Northern climates, it does not ripen its fruits beyond the fifty-fifth degree of North latitude.

Mons. Chas. Baltet, in his excellent treatise on the subject, gives descriptions and illustrations of the best varieties of Walnuts. Besides the common kind, he mentions and figures the *noix a coque tendre* or *noix a mesange*, a nut of medium size and elongated shape, the shell of which is easly detached from the kernel; the *noix a gros* fruit, of which there are several varieties with round or elongated nuts, desirable kinds, good for eating when freshly gathered; the *noix de la St. Jean*, a medium sized nut with a hard shell, the principal merit of the variety being that it is late in coming into growth, a point of some account in making a selection of varieties, as the Walnut suffers from late Spring frosts unless it is somewhat sheltered, and early growing sorts, of course, suffer the most.

Amongst the varieties grown in France, M. Baltet also mentions the Chaberte, Franquette, Mayette, Parisienne and Barthere, the last named being a very elongated, peculiar looking nut. Lastly, the Noyer Fertile (*juglans fertilis*), a variety highly recommended, which bears fruit at a very early age, and comes tolerably true from seed.

There are besides many varieties of ornamental foliaged Walnut trees well adapted for pleasure grounds and also yielding good fruit, such as *Juglans heterophylla, J. lanciniata*, and the Weeping Walnut (*J. pendula*), which when grafted as a tall standard forms a magnificent tree of most picturesque appearance.—ED. PYNAERT, in *Bulletin d'Arboriculture*.

*This is known in England as saddle grafting.

Varieties of Persian Walnuts.

As the Walnut is almost invariably propagated from seed and they do not exactly reproduce themselves, it is difficult to confine any variety to any distinct type.

BARTHERE.

CHABERTE.

Barthere.—A French variety; elongated; broad at the centre and tapering at each end.

Chaberte.—A French variety, and there cultivated largely for its oil; blooms late.

Franquette.—French; large; blooms late.

Mayette.—French. This is one of the finest dessert nuts and most highly prized in market; it also blooms late.

Parisienne—French; nut large; blooms late.

Praeparturiens.—(Fertile); size medium; shell rather hard; excellent quality; tree of dwarfish habit and bears very young; also blooms late.

FRANQUETTE.

MAYETTE.

PARISIENNE.

Kaghazi is claimed to be the hardiest of all soft shelled Walnuts and stands several degrees below zero without injury. It is a vigorous, free grower and transplants readily; very prolific, producing nuts in clusters and comes to fruiting very young. It puts out leaves and blossoms late in the Spring and thus escapes late frosts. The nut is larger than the ordinary varieties; the kernel full, plump, meaty; sweet, rich in oils and of fine flavor. The shell is thin.

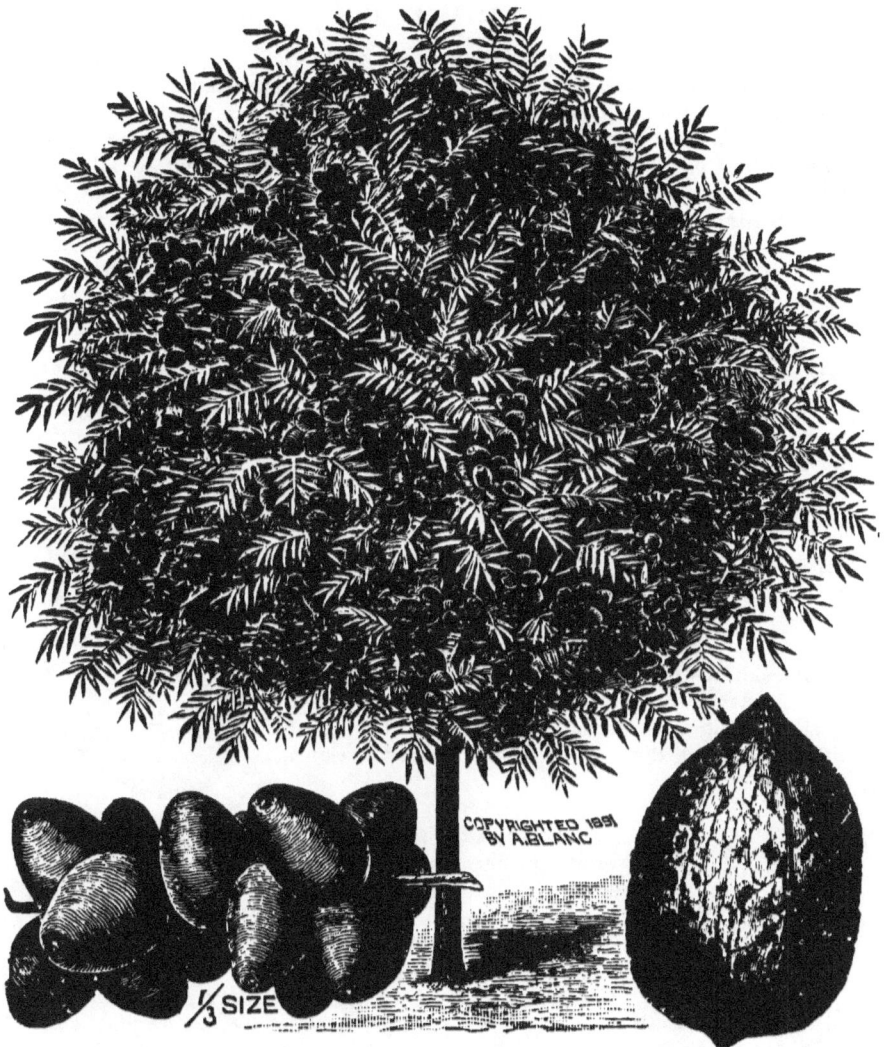

JAPAN WALNUT.

JAPAN WALNUTS.

The Japan Walnuts (*J. sieboldiana*), (*J. cordiformis*), (*J. mandshurica*), differ very little in habit of growth, foliage or general appearance, and may be described as vigorous growers, very hardy, assume a very handsome round head, mature early, bear young and are regular and abundant bearers. The trees make a more rapid growth than any other of the Walnut or Hickory family and are nicely adapted for roadside planting and in New Jersey are being used for this purpose. The leaves are of immense size and a charming shade of green.

These three varieties are all in fruiting at *Parrys' Pomona Nurseries*, and appear to reproduce themselves with wonderful accuracy. The nuts produced are apparently identical with those planted from which the trees were grown.

They have been widely distributed, succeeding admirably on the sandy soils of the Atlantic Coast from New York to Florida. Their mass of fibrous roots renders their transplanting as safe as that of an Apple or Orange, and their vigorous growth, with luxuriant foliage, will adapt them to the light sandy soils and hot climate of the Southern States.

Varieties

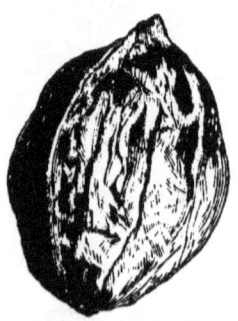

Juglans Sieboldiana.—This was probably the first of the Japan Walnuts introduced in this country. The oldest tree known was grown from seed planted about 1860 by *Mr. Towerhouse*, in Shasta Co., Cal. Nut ovate, sharp point. Shell thicker than that of Persian Walnut, but not so thick as American. Kernel, flavor of Butternut, less oily and better quality. Nuts are borne in clusters of twelve or fifteen each, at the top of the previous season's growth.

Juglans Cordiformis.—From the Island of Tezo, the most northern portion of the Japanese Empire, and should be entirely hardy throughout the United States. It has withstood a cold of several degrees below zero at Parrys' Pomona Nurseries, Parry, N. J., without the slightest injury. In form the tree is very similar to the foregoing and comes to fruiting at four years from seed. The nut is of peculiar heart shape, hence its name. Kernel full and plump, equaling in flavor the Persian Walnut; while its cracking qualities are superior to any other known varieties, as by boiling the nuts for about five minutes and cracking by a slight tap while still hot, the thin shells readily part and the kernel can be extracted whole, which feature will render them valuable. The meat is very sweet and will be much used by confectioners.

Juglans Mandschurica.—This species resembles the foregoing two in habit of growth and differing but little from the American Butternut. The nut is also more of the character of the Butternut, the shell being thick and rough.

CALIFORNIA BLACK WALNUT.

This tree is described as attaining a height of from fifty to seventy-five feet and two to four feet in diameter. Nut is round; kernel sweet and good flavor; shell smoother than the Eastern Black Walnut, though shell so thick as to render the nuts of little market value. The tree, however, may prove valuable as a stock on which to work the Persian Walnut in sections where the latter does not succeed.

SIBERIAN WALNUT.

From Meehan's Monthly.

It is said that the Siberian Walnut (*Pterocarya Caucasica*), has edible nuts of as much value as some other members of the Walnut family. The tree has been found quite hardy in the Northeastern parts of the United States; but so far as known, no specimen has fruited in this country. It differs from our ordinary Walnut and Hickory in having wings to the husks. It was this that suggested the name of *Pterocarya*.

A USEFUL INSECT.

From Meehan's Monthly.

Mr. P. H. Strubler, of Naperville, Ill., sends some Black Walnuts that have had the shells completely hollowed out by some insect, in an early stage. They have not entered through the shell to the seed, so that the Walnut is not in the least injured for edible purposes, but rather given an advantage, for after this skeletonizing by the insect the shell can be cracked with little more force than would have to be employed on a rather hard Almond.

COCOANUT.

The **Cocoanut** is adapted to but a very small area in this country. It is a native of tropical Africa and India, and recently has been extensively planted, by enterprising fruit growers of New Jersey, on the sea coast of Southern Florida.

It is a tall tree-like palm, attaining a height of seventy-five to one hundred feet and one to two feet in diameter, without branches. It has a tuft of about a dozen long pinnate leaves at the top, each with long strong mid-rib with leaflets on either side nearly three feet wide at the base and tapering to a point. The nuts are produced in clusters of a dozen or more, each encased in a husk of tough fibre. The nuts are utilized in a number of ways, the natives using the solid part as food and the milk as drink. They also are an extensive article of commerce, manufactured for many purposes.

Germination *Cocos nucifera* can be germinated from fresh seeds as follows: Take light, well-drained soil, and a pot ten to twelve inches in diameter; lay the nut on its side when planting, and cover it about two-thirds only; do not remove the outer husk. The pot should be plunged in bottom heat of at least seventy-five or eighty degrees. It requires sometimes from two to three months to germinate.—N. BUTTERBACH.

THE COCOANUT IN FLORIDA.

From Florists' Exchange.

The introduction of this valuable tree in Florida, where, although very abundant it is not indigenous, was due to the wreck, near Jupiter Inlet, of a vessel from Bahama loaded with Cocoanuts.

The nuts that were cast ashore were immediately planted by the residents on that then sparsely populated part of the country and were found to thrive wonderfully, and now in Dade county, in the southernmost part of the State, having a sea front of one hundred and fifty miles, are many Cocoanut groves of from one hundred to six thousand trees.

The trees make a most beautiful and imposing grove, being truly tropical in their appearance. As they are planted only about twenty feet apart, they cast a thick, unvarying shade. They are evergreen, as is most tropical foliage, and their gracefulness, with the great height they attain, makes them a desirable addition to a home in the far South. The diameter of the tree ranges from one foot to four, and they attain a height of one hundred and twenty-five feet, having as many as four hundred nuts on them at one time.

These beautiful palms add greatly to the attractive appearance of the tropics, the long feathery leaves that undulate so gracefully in the breeze which sighs among them, the "everlasting green" of their coloring, their tall stateliness and their symmetry, beautify the whole country where they grow—especially Southern Florida, where they grow in such profusion.

The Cocoanut tree begins bearing six years after the planting of the ripe nut, and after that time it is never without fruit in all stages of growth. It continues bearing for about twenty-five years and after the first year, during which it needs protection from the wind, its cultivation gives no trouble.

PEANUT; GROUNDNUT.

This nut is extensively grown in the Atlantic Coast States, thriving in the low, moist, sandy grounds, and is a very important crop in Virginia.

PEANUT CULTIVATION.

By Dr. John Morris, in Baltimore News.

There is a new industry now being introduced in the State of Washington which might be successfully initiated in our own State, viz: The cultivation of the Peanut. From experiments in Germany it has been ascertained that the Peanut contains more nutritive material than any other form of food, more than milk, butter, eggs, lard, bacon, beef, etc. The American Peanut contains forty-two per cent. of oil. The Germans express this and sell it at about sixty cents a gallon. It is sweet and nutritious and much better for salads than the cotton-seed oil which we import from Italy under the name of olive oil. After expressing the oil the Germans prepare four forms of food from the Peanut. Flour, which contains the husk, etc.; grits, similar to our preparation of corn; plain biscuits and a diabetic biscuit which, being free from sugar, is used in cases of diabetes.

RECIPES.

ALMONDS.

To Blanch Almonds.

Shell them, immerse in boiling water and let stand five minutes; then dip in cold water and the skins can be easily removed with the fingers.

To Salt Almonds.

Shell them, blanch and spread out thin on plate; stir through a small quantity of butter and place in slow oven to brown. Take them from the oven, sprinkle with salt, and stir till thoroughly coated and turn out onto a cloth to cool.

Almond Macaroons.

From Philadelphia Press.

One pound of pulverized sugar, three eggs, one pint of nuts rolled fine, one saucer of flour. Mix sugar and yolks, add whites, well beaten, and lastly flour. Drop with a spoon. Leave space for spreading.

MRS. W. G. G.

SHENANDOAH, PA.

Macaroons.

From Philadelphia Press.

Margery Daw's recipe for hickory macaroons is as follows (I suppose almonds could be substituted in much the same proportion): One pound powdered sugar, one pound of nuts, chopped fine, the unbeaten whites of five eggs, one tablespoonful flour, two small teaspoonfuls of baking powder. Mix these ingredients together and drop from a spoon upon buttered paper or baking tins. Do not put them too near each other, and bake a light brown in a moderate oven. Weigh nuts before cracking.

BETSY TROTWOOD.

CITY, March 1.

Almond Macaroons.

From Philadelphia Press.

Two eggs, whites, one coffee cup level full of powdered sugar, one-half pound of sweet Almonds. Pour boiling water over the Almonds to take off the brown skin, then put them in the oven to dry; when cold pound them to paste. Beat up the eggs and sugar to a stiff froth and add them to the Almond paste, mixing them thoroughly with the back of a spoon. Roll the preparation in your hands in little balls the size of a nutmeg and place them on a piece of white paper an inch apart. Bake them in a cool oven a light brown.

MRS. H. J. S.

HARRISBURG, February 9.

Reception Cake.

Two cupfuls of butter, two cupfuls of sugar, ten eggs, one quart of flour, one teaspoonful baking powder, two cupfuls currants, cupful citron, in thin small slices; one-half orange rind, peeled very thin and cut small; one-half cupful Almonds, blanched and cut in shreds; one teaspoonful each extract of allspice and cinnamon. Rub the butter and sugar to a white light cream, add the eggs, two at a time, beating five minutes between each addition. Add the flour sifted with the powder, currants, citron, orange peel, Almonds and extracts. Mix carefully into a rather soft batter, put in a buttered paper-lined shallow cake tin, bake carefully in a moderate steady oven two and one-quarter hours.

MRS. JNO. CHEESMAN.

CAMDEN, N. J.

Almond Balls.

Two cups sugar, three-fourths cup cold water, boil until it hairs. Set away to cool for half an hour, and then add a half pound blanched almonds broken in small pieces, and a few drops of either vanilla or bitter almonds, according to taste. Stir with a wooden spoon until it creams; place on a marble slab or a large dish and knead a few minutes as you would bread; then mould into balls with your hands.

Fruit Cake.

Two pounds raisins, one pound currants, five ounces citron, five ounces orange peel, six ounces lemon peel, one-half pound almonds, one pound butter, one pound brown sugar, one-half dozen eggs well beaten, two tablespoonfuls mace, one tablespoonful cinnamon, two grated nutmegs, one pound sifted flour. Dissolve one tablespoonful of baking soda in a little water before putting in oven; bake two hours in slow oven.

MRS. CLYDE.

COCOANUT.

Cream Cocoanut Pudding.

Two cups grated cocoanut, four tablespoonfuls cornstarch, one teaspoonful vanilla, one pint milk, four eggs, one-half cup sugar. Put milk in farina boiler, moisten cornstarch in a little cold milk, then add it to the boiling milk, stir until smooth, beat the whites of the eggs to a very stiff froth, add the sugar to the pudding, then the whites, beat well over fire for three minutes, now add cocoanut and vanilla and turn into mould to harden; serve with vanilla sauce.

MRS. THOMAS EDWARD STEELE.

Cream Cocoanut

Two pounds confectioners' sugar, one-quarter pound shredded cocoanut, whites of two eggs, beaten; one-half teaspoonful extract vanilla, enough sweet cream to make a stiff dough.

Cocoanut Bar.

Four cups of sugar, one cup of water, one-half teaspoonful of cream of tarter, one-quarter pound of cocoanut. Stir the sugar, water and cream of tarter together until the sugar is dissolved, as soon as bubbles are seen; cook without stirring for several minutes. Remove immediately from the range, Cool (but in a very cold place); then beat until it thickens, and add the cocoanut. Dessicated cocoanut may be used. Spread on buttered pans, cool, but not in a cold place, as it hardens the top. It should be soft and creamy, and may be cut into bars at any time.

CHESTNUTS.

To Blanch Chestnuts.

Remove the shells, place the nuts in boiling water and let remain ten to fifteen minutes; pour off the water and the brown skin will readily slip from the kernel. Then the Chestnuts are ready for use in any recipe.

MRS. WM. PARRY.

Stewed Chestnuts.

Blanch the Chestnuts, boil fifteen minutes, add a teaspoonful of salt for one quart of Chestnuts and boil five to ten minutes longer, or until they can be pierced with a fork. Remove from the pan, drain and cover with cream sauce or drawn butter.

MRS. JOHN R. PARRY.

To Stuff Chicken With Chestnuts.

Roast one quart of large Chestnuts, shell and mash. Take one-half and add a tablespoonful of butter, a teaspoonful of salt and dash of pepper; thoroughly mix and fill the chicken. With wooden toothpicks pin thin slices of salt pork to the breast of the chicken and place it in the pan; pour in a half cupful of water and half teaspoonful of salt. In roasting allow one hour to four pounds, basting frequently. When done remove the chicken and put in the pan the balance of the Chestnuts. Add one-half pint of stock, salt and pepper to taste and stir until it boils. For **Roast Turkey** use double the quantity of Chestnuts.

Turkey Stuffing.

From Philadelphia Press.

Our Christmas turkey stuffing was much liked. It is as follows: For a sixteen pound turkey we used two quarts of large Chestnuts and one loaf of stale bread. Some of the bread was put in the breast, the remainder used for the large cavity. Boil Chestnuts with a pinch of salt in the water, shell and remove brown skin, chop, sprinkle with celery salt, crumble bread, add a small lump of butter, salt to taste, chop ends of celery (about one stalk.) The bread used for breast can be flavored with thyme, sage or parsley, celery and a little pepper. If turkey is well basted the dressing will be moist and better flavored.

MRS. L. J. K. FOWDEN.

ATLANTIC CITY, Jan. 11.

Chestnut Stuffing for Birds.

From Philadelphia Press.

Chestnut forcemeat is made as follows: Place a saucepan with one tablespoonful fine chopped onion and two ounces butter over the fire, cook five minutes, without browning; add six ounces fine chopped fresh pork from the loin or tenderloin; add twelve fine chopped mushrooms, twelve finely pounded cooked Chestnuts; stir and cook five minutes longer; remove from the fire; season with one teaspoonful salt, one-half teaspoonful pepper and one-half pound whole peeled and cooked Chestnuts, three tablespoonfuls of bread crumbs, mix all together. Another way is to boil one pound of peeled Chestnuts in milk till tender, then pound them fine and mix with two ounces butter, a little salt and pepper and use for stuffing, or mix with this puree four ounces sausage meat and one ounce butter. This can be used for all sorts of birds or poultry.

MARTHA.

TRENTON.

Cooked Chestnuts—as Requested.

From Philadelphia Press.

Take one quart of Chestnuts, shell them, then scald them and take off the skin, put the Chestnuts on to boil with a little salt, then put in one and one-half pounds of prunes, one-quarter pound of raisins, same of currants; slice one or two onions into this and sugar to sweeten, and some lemon juice. Then add a dip of flour and water and a little cinnamon and you will find this very fine, as I have given this recipe to many friends. As I have used a great many recipes from your column I thought I would send you one. More may follow. If you wish any information I will send you some through your columns which I read every day.

MRS. B. B.

CALLOWHILL.

Purée of Chestnuts.

By Mrs. Rorer, in Ladies' Home Journal.

Shell and blanch one quart of Chestnuts. Put them in a soup kettle and cover with one quart of stock; add a slice of onion, two bay leaves, a quarter of a teaspoonful of celery seed or half a cup of chopped celery tops. Cook slowly for twenty minutes until the Chestnuts are tender. Press through a colander first, then through a sieve. Return the puree to the kettle, add a pint of milk. Rub together two tablespoonfuls of butter and one of flour; stir into the hot puree, stirring constantly for five minutes; add a teaspoonful and a half of salt and half a teaspoonful of pepper. Press again through the sieve, reheat, and it will be ready to serve.

White Purée of Chestnuts.

From Philadelphia Inquirer.

Take a hundred Chestnuts and make a slit across the top of each to prevent their bursting. Melt two and a half ounces of butter in a clean stewpan. Put in the Chestnuts, and fry them gently until the husks come off easily. Now remove all skin and brown them. Put them into a saucepan, with one quart of milk and water mixed together in equal proportions. Add one small onion, one stick of celery, the white part only, and one small cleaned carrot cut in half only. Simmer all these gently till the Chestnuts are quite soft. Drain off all the liquid and remove the onion, celery and carrot. Pound the Chestnuts till smooth, then rub them through a hair sieve. Add some of the liquid in which they were boiled as you put them through the sieve; it makes them work easier. When all is rubbed through, add any milk and water you may have left out and one other quart of milk as well. Reboil this, stirring all the time. Then let it simmer gently by the side of the stove and keep it well skimmed. Just before serving it season with pepper, salt, a few grains of sugar, and pour in half a pint of thick cream. Serve with fried bits of bread.

HICKORY NUTS.

Nut Cake.

Two cups of sugar, one cup of butter, one cup of milk, three eggs, two and one-half to three cups of flour, two teaspoonfuls of Rumford's yeast powder and two cups of any kind of nut kernels.

MRS. F. ANDERSON.

Nut Cake.

Four eggs, two cups sugar, one cup milk, one-half cup butter, three cups flour, two cups Hickory nuts, two teaspoonfuls baking powder, flavor with almond or lemon. Beat sugar and butter to cream, then add eggs, well beaten; add milk; mix baking powder and flour and add; beat well, then add nuts sprinkled with flour. Last, flavor. Cook in moderate oven.

MRS. H. M. ROYAL.

Nut Salad.
From Philadelphia Press.

The recipe for nut salad is as follows: Crack, pick kernels and chop enough mixed nuts to have a cupful of kernels; chop fine one stalk of celery (using only the white part, saving ends with leaves for garnishing); sprinkle some celery salt, pinch of table salt and mix all with three or four tablespoonfuls of prepared meat dressing (any brand you prefer), or mayonnaise or a slaw dressing. This can be served on salad or lettuce leaves, a small quantity being put on each leaf, or it can be garnished with the ends of the celery stuck upright in the salad bowl. The quantities given make sufficient for six persons.

MRS. L. J. K. FOWDEN.

ATLANTIC CITY, February 4.

Dainty Nut Sandwiches.
From Philadelphia Press.

Chop the nuts very fine, making a mixture of one-half Almonds, one-quarter English Walnuts and the remainder Hickory nuts. Butter the bread, slice, put on it a thin layer of the chopped nuts, a dust of salt, a sprinkle of grated cheese and cover with another slice.

GASTRONOMIC.

ALLENTOWN, October 27.

Hickory-Nut Macaroons.

In response to our request for a recipe for Hickory-nut Macaroons, we have received a number of replies, from which we select the following as differing from others, and also recommended as having been tried and found successful:

Two cupfuls of finely-chopped hickory-nut meats, two eggs, four tablespoonfuls of sifted flour, one cupful of sifted, pulverized sugar; flavor with almond extract. Beat the eggs very light, beating in the flour slowly, then the sugar by spoonfuls. Add the meats last. Bake on buttered paper in a slow oven.

MRS. CHAS. STRICKLAND.

One cupful of chopped nuts, one cupful of pulverized sugar, one egg (yolk and white beaten separately), one tablespoonful of flour. Mix the nuts and sugar, then the yolk, then the white, and lastly the flour. Accuracy is very essential in measuring these ingredients.

MRS. G. T. ANDREWS.

Beat the whites of five eggs to a stiff froth, then add one pound of pulverized sugar, one pound of kernels chopped, and two tablespoonfuls of flour. Drop half tablespoonfuls of the batter on a sheetiron pan, and bake in a quick oven.

MRS. J. B. MOSTELLER.

Hickory Nut Cake.

Whites of three eggs, one-half pound of pulverized sugar, one-half pound of hickory nut kernels, one teaspoonful of vanilla, three scant tablespoonfuls of flour.

MRS. WIGGINS.

Nut Cake—Excellent.

Two cups sugar, one cup butter, four eggs, three and one-half cups flour, two teaspoonfuls baking powder, one cup milk, one cup chopped raisins, one cup cut-up English Walnuts, one teaspoon vanilla.

Shellbark Cake.

One scant cup of butter, two cups of sugar, one cup of milk, three even cupfuls of flour, whites of six eggs, or three whole eggs beaten separately, two teaspoonfuls baking powder. Cream, butter and sugar, add milk, gradually stir in the flour and baking powder, then whites of eggs and lastly one cup of Shellbark kernels, chopped fine, stirred in gently. Bake in pound cake mould.

MRS. F. B. WISECANER.

PEANUTS.

Palatable Peanuts.

SINCE PHYSICIANS HAVE DECLARED THE NUT NUTRITIOUS, IT IS POPULAR.
From Philadelphia Press.

There was a time when peanuts were doomed to fairs and the circus, and were supposed to belong by right to only the small boy and girl.

Now this heretofore "vulgar" nut is very popular, and all sorts of palatable things are made with it, for physicians say that the peanut is "an article of food rich in albumen, of which it contains fifty per cent., with twenty per cent. of fat and non-nitrogenous extractive matters." The Chinese boil the Peanuts, roll them fine, mold them into dough and bake them. Peanuts make fine sandwiches.

One way of making them is to roll the meats very fine and stir them thickly in mayonnaise dressing and spread between thin slices of bread. Another method is to roll or pound the shelled and skinned Peanuts and spread them thickly upon thin slices of buttered bread.

Sprinkle lightly with salt before putting the slices together. Still another filling is made by salting the powdered nut meats and mixing them with enough cream cheese to hold them together. Spread this on squares of thin bread or crackers. These sandwiches are particularly nice to serve with lettuce salad.

Peanut soup is made like a dried pea soup. Soak one and one-half pints of nut meats over night in two quarts of water. In the morning add three quarts of water, a bay leaf, a stalk of celery, a blade of mace, and one slice of onion. Boil this slowly for four or five hours, stirring frequently to prevent burning.

Rub through a sieve and return to the fire. When again hot add one cup of cream. Let the soup boil up once and it is ready to serve. Serve croutons of bread with this soup. Peanut meringue shells are nice to serve with plain ice cream.

Beat the whites of four eggs very light and stir in three-quarters of a pound of powdered sugar, one tablespoonful of flour, and one cup of finely chopped Peanuts. Drop the mixture by the spoonful upon buttered papers and bake in a rather cool oven.

Place a shell on each side of a large spoonful of ice cream and put a little whipped cream over the top in serving.

Peanut Candy.

One cup granulated sugar, one cup rolled Peanuts. The Peanuts are prepared by chopping or by rolling with a wooden pin. Heat the sugar in a hot oven; when it has melted remove to back of range and add the Peanuts, mixing them thoroughly with the sugar. Spread on a tin and press into shape with knives. The tin does not need greasing. Cut into bars. It hardens immediately.

O. K. S.

PECANS.

Mrs. McKee's Cake.

SHE VOUCHES FOR THE EXCELLENCY OF THIS PECAN DELICACY.

From Philadelphia Press.

Mrs. McKee, daughter of ex-President Harrison, vouches for the perfection of a recipe for making Pecan cake. Beat together a cup of butter and two of sugar, adding a little beaten white of egg; then put in a cup of flour, a half cup of sweet milk, then another cup of flour. The last flour must contain two teaspoonfuls of baking powder. Add the whites of eight eggs (allowing for that which has been taken from them to mix with the butter and sugar). The filling and icing is made as follows: Two cups of nuts should soak awhile in a grated pineapple, after chopping them fine. Now mix them (first lightly flour the chopped Pecans) into the whites (beaten stiff) of six eggs and powdered sugar. Put whole Pecan kernels over the top of the cake while the icing is still soft.

WALNUTS.

English Walnut Filling For Cake.

Two scant cups of sugar, two-thirds of a cup of milk, butter size of an egg. Put all over the fire, and when at the boiling point add one-half pound of English Walnuts, chopped fine; let all boil five or ten minutes, stirring constantly; add two teaspoonfuls of vanilla. Beat until cool and thick enough to spread.

A. R. REEVES.

Walnut Cakes.

From Philadelphia Press.

Chop very fine or put through a meat cutter sufficient nuts to make one and one-half cupfuls when prepared. Separate the whites and yolks of five eggs and beat the yolks with three-quarters of a cupful of powdered sugar.

When very light add four tablespoonfuls of flour and the walnut meal, one teaspoonful of vanilla and the stiffly-beaten whites of the eggs. Stir in one-half of a teaspoonful of baking powder and pour into a shallow baking pan; the batter should not be over one inch in depth. Bake in a moderate oven. When cold cut into diamonds, square or circles and dip into melted fondant slightly flavored with vanilla. Before this sets press in the centre of each cake an unbroken half of a walnut.

Lancaster. L. S. S.

Bonbons from Betsy Trotwood.

French cream candy is made without cooking. The secret is in the sugar used, which is the XXX powdered or confectioners' sugar. Ordinary powdered sugar when rubbed between the thumb and finger has a decided grain, but the confectioners' sugar is as fine as flour.

French Vanilla Cream.

Break into a bowl the white of one egg, add an equal quantity of cold water; then stir in XXX powdered or confectioners' sugar until stiff enough to mould into shape with the fingers. Flavor with vanilla to taste. After it is formed into the desired shapes lay upon plates or waxed paper and set aside to dry. This cream is the foundation for all the French creams.

English Walnut Creams.

Make French cream. Have ready some English Walnuts, taking care not to break the meats. Make a ball of the cream about the size of a Walnut and place a half nut meat upon either side of the ball, pressing them into the cream. Lay aside a few hours to dry.

Cream Dates.

Select perfect Dates and with a knife remove the pit. Take a piece of French cream, make an oblong shape and wrap the Date around the cream. Another method for making French cream is to use ordinary white sugar and to boil it. Four cups white sugar and one cup of hot water are placed in a bright tin pan on the range and boiled without stirring for about eight minutes; if it looks somewhat stiff test by letting some drop from the spoon, and if it threads remove the pan to the table, taking small spoonful and rubbing it against the side of a cake bowl. If creamy and will roll into a ball between the fingers, pour the whole into the bowl and beat rapidly with a large spoon or porcelain potato masher. If it is not boiled enough to cream set it back upon the range, let it remain one or two minutes, or as long as necessary, taking care not to cook it too much. Add vanilla (or other flavoring) as soon as it begins to cool. These candies are from Margery Daw's little book.

BETSY TROTWOOD.

INDEX.

	PAGE.
ALMONDS	47
Diseases	49
Insects and diseases	49
Varieties	50
American Institute, notes from	77
BEECH, Propagation	50
Budding	41
Budding and grafting	41
CHESTNUTS, American	51
Budding and grafting	80
Culture, C. Parry	56
Culture, R. N. Yorker	74
Cultivation, R. N. Yorker	63
Crop	59
European	85
European varieties	85
Food value	54
Grafting	42
Grafting in N. E.	75
Grafting on oaks, R. N. Yorker	81
How to destroy worms in	83
In California, by Felix Gillet	66
Insect enemies	82
Japan	88
Paragon, by J. S. Woodward	60
Paragon	61
Preparation for market	80

INDEX.

	PAGE.
CHESTNUTS, propagation	80
Trees grafted	79
Varieties	84
CHINQUAPINS, Varieties	91
COCOANUTS, Germination	142
In Florida	142
Florida Fruits	129
Grafting, Wax	44
Wax, liquid	45
Grafts, Care of	44
HAZELNUTS, American	91
Propagation	92
Varieties	92
HICKORIES	92
Others	119
Nut Culture	24
Culture, history of, in North America	7
Culture for New York	11
Growing in Sonoma County	126
Nuts, a bag of	27
Germination of	32
Propagation of	32
Wild and cultivated	20
Nut trees, a plea for	17
How to plant	36
Trees and plants, care of	33
Trees, distances for planting	35
Oaks, Hickories and Walnuts	128
Orchard culture	46
PEANUTS	143
PECANS	93
Acreage in Florida	112
And English Walnuts	114
And their culture	109
And Fruit culture	98
Budding and grafting	95
Culture	96
Enemies	117
Grafting	112
Growing in Louisiana	102

INDEX. 157

	PAGE.
PECANS, Growing in Kansas	116
Growing in Tennessee	111
Growing in Missouri	115
Propagation	94
Raising	113
Raising in Texas	107
Varieties	117
RECIPES, Almonds	144
Cocoanut	146
Chestnut	146
Hickory nut	149
Peanut	151
Pecan	152
Walnut	152
SHELLBARKS, Grafting	118
Varieties	119
WALNUTS, Black and Butternuts	120, 125
California black	141
Growing in Central and Northern California	122
Hulls	131
In Europe	131
Japan	139
Japan varieties	140
Native	120
Persian	121
Persian varieties	137
Propagation (Native)	120
Propagation (Persian)	121
Siberian	141
The Common	134
Useful insect	141

www.ingramcontent.com/pod-product-compliance
Lightning Source LLC
Chambersburg PA
CBHW030310170426
43202CB00009B/942